God's Whispered Dreams: Messages, Meanings, and Miracles

Mari Fitz-Wynn

I0623396

Copyright and Bible Permission Page

God's Whispered Dreams: Messages, Meanings, and Miracles
Copyright 2024 by Faith Journey Publishing

All rights reserved. No portion of this book may be reproduced, stored in a retrieval system, or transmitted in any form or by any means—electronic, mechanical, photocopy, recording, or other—except in the case of brief quotations embodied in critical and certain other non-commercial uses permitted by copyright law, reviews, without the prior permission of the publisher. For permission requests, please address Faith Journey Publishing, LLC.

Published 2024
Printed in the United States of America
ISBN: 979-8-9858168-6-0

Cover design by Nicki Black
South Main Media

For information, contact:
Faith Journey Publishing, LLC
contact@faithjourneypublishing.com

Scripture quotations marked AMP are taken from The Amplified® Bible, Copyright© 2015 by The Lockman Foundation. Used by permission. (www.Lockman.org) All rights reserved.

Scripture quotations marked ESV are taken from The Holy Bible, English Standard Version® (ESV®), Copyright© 2001, 2016 by Crossway, a publishing ministry of Good News Publishers. Used by permission. All rights reserved.

Scriptures marked KJV are taken from the King James Version of the Bible. Public Domain.

Scriptures marked NIV are taken from the Holy Bible, New International Version®, NIV®. Copyright© 1973, 1978, 1984, 2011 by Biblica, Inc.™ Used by permission of Zondervan. All rights reserved worldwide. www.zondervan.com "NIV" and "New International Version" are trademarks registered in the United States Patent and Trademark Office by Biblica, Inc.™

Scriptures marked NLT are taken from the Holy Bible, New Living Translation, copyright©1996, 2004, 2015 by Tyndale House Foundation. Used by permission of Tyndale House Publishers, Inc., Carol Stream, Illinois 60188. All rights reserved.

Dreams are not about what we want, but what the Holy Spirit desires to accomplish through them.
—M.F-W.

Table of Contents

Introduction 1

Chapter 1: The Legacy..6

Chapter 2: The Problem...11

Chapter 3: The Answer 16

Chapter 4: The Dreams...22

Chapter 5: The Gift 33

Chapter 6: The Talk 38

Chapter 7: The Skeptics 44

Chapter 8: The Keys 54

Chapter 9: The Dreamer 57

Chapter 10: The Interpretation...................................62

Chapter 11: Types of Dreams......................................74

Learning to Interpret 89

Testimonials of Dreams and Visions 93

FAQs..98

Appendix of Dreams and Visions 101

Endnotes...139

Introduction

From nightmares to a vivid, spectra-colored, image-rich world, our every dream is about victory. The foe may be a mini alligator with enormous teeth or creatures or humans chasing in hot pursuit when we leap victoriously to the sky or disappear at the last possible second. Victory comes as we answer a seemingly impossible question or puzzle presented through the entire dream. Alternatively, one moment our dreams may put us in chaotic, crowded surroundings then sweep us away to a place of ultimate serenity, peace, and beauty. Supernaturally, we are bridged between the ethereal and the spiritual. Our dreams serve as windows to victory in both our daily and spiritual life. Once the interpretation comes, we understand the connection between dreams and God's purpose, love, and wisdom.

God's message to us through our dreams is sometimes simple, sometimes complicated, but it is always an expression of His great love and concern for every area of our lives. While hard to understand as it is happening before our eyes, a dream has a foundational principle applicable to God's Word—not to be made to fit His Word but to reveal His truth. This truth can only be applied through the godly wisdom and discernment given to those gifted to interpret dreams.

The reality of dreams is not limited to what we read from Genesis to Revelation; dreams did not end with the Bible. God still gives dreams in the 21st century, and those willing to listen to His instruction, warning, encouragement, or revelation in their dreams build a bridge to strengthen communication or develop a higher level of relationship with the Trinity.

A few years ago, I dreamed about writing a book about dreams. Many books and other resources about dreams exist, and this posed a dilemma because I still wanted to write a book about dreams, specifically mine. I put the book project idea aside for several months. Eventually, I realized that no matter how many other books had been written on the subject, I was the only one who could write a book about my dreams. The Lord clarified this point by giving me a dream so specific—outlining from start to finish the order by chapters and how the book was to be arranged. The content was also given—my experience as a dreamer, the dreams and visions of the Spirit, and a biblical perspective on a few of the dreams and dreamers we find in the Bible. All I had to do was sit down, write, and be mindful of the distractions that could hinder me from completing the book.

The Dream That Became This Book

In the dream, I am on the phone with my friend Dixie. At my feet are two kittens, one purple and one beige. Both are very annoying. They aren't trying to attack but are vying to get my attention, and they are a distraction the entire time I am on the phone.

Our conversation in the dream:

M: I think you need to write a section on dream interpretation.

D: No. Why would I do that?

M: People will want to know if they have the gift of interpretation.

D: Okay.

M: Get back! Go away! (to the kittens)

M: You could also include how it happens, getting it right away, or sometimes taking a while. Remember when you'd say, "I don't have anything on your dream yet. Let me take it to the Lord"?

D: Oh, yeah.

M: That's for the people who won't get an interpretation immediately and doubt they have the gift. (Simultaneously, I am trying to get away from the cats.)

D: Hello? Hello?

The dream ended.

Interpretation: Dixie

This dream advances the purpose that the Lord wants this book written and has given Mari the desire to do it, and it will include a section on the principles of interpreting dreams. The cats, not attacking Mari but aggravating her, represent those who will try to distract her from this endeavor. She will have to deal with and isolate them so they cannot distract her or have any upsetting influence as she writes the book.

Chapter 1: The Legacy

As a young girl, sometimes I told my dreams to others, but often I felt too shy, so I kept them to myself.

My grandmother was a dreamer. Now and then, my mother and aunts would have dreams too. In my naïveté, I believed everyone —every kid and their families—had the same experience. We all had dreams and lots of them.

As a girl, I heard many conversations about someone's dream and how it came true. My childhood experiences revolved around these stories, not only those of my relatives but also those of the people at our church who frequently shared their dreams. I enjoyed listening to them. Given that I believed everyone dreamed, I also thought dreaming was nothing special.

I should note here that I was never surprised when what I dreamed happened. I expected no less because my grandmother's dreams came to pass. This actuality formed my foundational belief that God could, through a dream, show us what would happen. Growing up, I learned dreams meant God was communicating with us—too heady a concept for a small child to comprehend. I went through childhood without completely understanding how vital and unique His communication could be. I did not think it was important.

Dreaming was not a big deal to me; after all, didn't everyone dream?

Childhood Dreams

Not long after my family moved into an all-white neighborhood, I dreamed a house was on fire, and there was so much smoke I started coughing to the point of choking, and it woke me up. Sitting up in my bed, trying to catch my breath, I realized my bedroom was filled with smoke! I looked out the window and saw flames shooting toward my room. Someone had set the garage of our new home on fire. My bedroom was next to the garage. I ran to wake my parents, who were soundly asleep in another part of the house.

During the ensuing years, I seemed to have a dream pattern that followed along the lines of tragedy and death. My night visions (dreams) grew more intense and, in my estimation, worse. During my college days, I dreamed more about people dying, only to learn about their deaths the following day, week, month, or even a year from the time of the dream. These night visions became such a burden. Not only that, but they also caused me to fear going to sleep.

Not all my dreams were tragic, though. As a matter of fact, one of the first dreams I had after I became a Christian occurred during a crisis. Several months after my college graduation, I was still looking for a job—any job. I had abandoned the hope of finding employment in my field of study. I prayed for direction on where to apply for a job. Still, no answer came. But one night, I had a dream.

Dream
I am boarding the city bus, and sitting right at the front is a friend from high school named Karen.

That's it.
I started my job hunt again the following day and stood at the bus stop. By now, you've probably guessed that I boarded the bus, paid my fare, and saw my friend Karen sitting in the front seat.

You may not be surprised, but I was! My dream came to mind immediately.

After I paid my fare, Karen invited me to sit with her. I was overly excited and just blurted out that I'd had a dream about her the night before. She did not know what to do with that information, and unfortunately, neither did I. We had a bit of awkward silence and then returned to our conversation.

We laughed and chatted, catching up with what had happened since we'd last seen each other. When I mentioned I was job hunting— going downtown to put in what felt like the hundredth job application and feeling desperate—she said her former employer planned to post a position that day. She urged me to go directly to see the manager, who was also a personal friend, and apply immediately, using her as a reference. I completed the paperwork and started my new job a few days later!

I never had the chance to bring the dream up in conversation with Karen again; our paths never crossed, but I wondered for a long time if she ever made the connection between my seeing her in a dream and then seeing her in person.

Even though there were a few dreams of good things, now and then, they never seemed to balance out with the number of hard ones. Looking back, now that I understand, the dreams of death or tragedy were the Lord's mercy to warn me and give me time to prepare emotionally for loss and to pray.

I learned and relearned that God's messages are not intended to harm us but to protect us.

Chapter 2: The Problem

Not long after I finished graduate school, I married. I must admit being a wife who dreamed had terrific advantages. For instance, I always had a captive audience and a witness to events I had dreamed about. Initially, I did not find in my husband, Edward, a ready believer in dreams. He grew up with the "What did you eat for dinner?" theology about dreams and questioned my or anyone else's possession of any gift of dreaming.

Poor fellow, he was in for a wild ride and didn't even know it.

Police Cruiser Dream

One morning as Edward headed into his home office, and I hurried off to work, the memory of a dream lingered—a hazy specter tugging at the edge of my thoughts. The image of a police cruiser, its slow roll down the street and its intentional stop in front of our house, was etched into my mind. There was something unsettling about the way the dream had ended, unresolved.

I couldn't shake off the feeling of unease as I settled into my office. The weight of the dream was pressing, and God was urging

11

me to share it with Edward. My fingers tapped the familiar numbers on the phone, and with a sense of urgency, I recounted the dream to him. "I don't know what else happened because I woke up," I told him.

His response, though, was oddly nonchalant. "Don't worry about it," he said, his voice lacking the apprehension I felt. His assurance should have been comforting, but instead his next words came in a rush. "I'm sure I can tell you what happened when I call you back. A police car just pulled up to the house."

At that time, a single mom and her children lived in the lower level of our home, and unbeknownst to us, there had been a breakdown in communication between her and her husband, and he'd sent the police to do a welfare check on his children.

Where Are the Good Dreams?

After we started our family, I noticed how my loved ones shuddered if I announced I had a dream the previous night. Not at all encouraging. My young daughter asked me once, "Don't you ever have any good dreams?"

"Yes," I answered feebly, as we both struggled to remember when and what it may have been.

The negativism did not stop with her. Sometimes, I told a few close friends about a dream, not necessarily one about them, but just a dream in general. They often made comments like, "Please don't dream about me," or they would rapidly change the subject—even less encouragement. I felt embarrassed, and sometime hurt. Eventually, I became self-conscious about mentioning the word *dream*. And I resented the sobering dreams.

I wanted dreams that would be fun to tell—ones that would gain other people's favor, or at least acceptance. But that is not how it works. Dreams are not about what we want, but what the Holy Spirit desires to accomplish through them.

I can't say I liked it one bit.

In one dream, I saw a house with lights on in every room. I recognized it as the home of a lady from my church. The voices were loud and contentious. I told her the dream, and her angry response was, "Every couple argues now and then." I knew this to be true, but why did the Lord show me the interior of her home? I thought perhaps the dream would encourage her to pray and find out. Instead, she was angry. Weeks passed before she could look me in the face. Months later, she finally broke her silence and apologized with an explanation of what she'd been going through before I shared my dream.

Subsequently, discouragement and bitterness formed in my heart. I stopped sharing my dreams because I did not learn soon enough that there can be a positive interpretation associated with an upsetting dream. I believed the lie from the Satan that no one wanted to hear or accept my dreams.

People often began a conversation with me about their dreams in this manner: "I had a horrible dream last night," or "I had a nightmare recently." Knowing that feeling, I would nod empathetically. I used to feel the same way and expressed it similarly.

I asked the Lord to stop. No. More. Dreams.

For a season, that is what happened: I lived in a dream desert. Now and then I dreamed, but just like a mirage, the dream disappeared from memory when I awoke.

Morning after morning, I woke up knowing there had been a dream and was pleased I could not recall it. I should have cared, but I didn't. I was experiencing a newfound freedom, even if it was tinged with guilt. I did not understand I was walking in total indifference to God's gift and plan for how He wanted to use dreams and visions in my life.

So, how did I circle back and come to a thankful place for my dreams and write a book about it, no less? Simple, I came face-to-face with my rebellious attitude.

Chapter 3: The Answer

I embarked on what became a transformative journey when I traveled to Chattanooga in 2012 to visit my spiritual mentor.

One evening, our discussion changed to the subject of dreams, and she asked about a dream I'd had a couple of years ago. The dream was literal. It concerned a mutual friend, and the outcome had been a warning about this friend's need to make some lifestyle changes. We continued our conversation, and then my mentor asked, "Have you had any other dreams lately?"

I proudly admitted, "No, I only dream sporadically. I've asked the Lord to stop them."

I will never forget the look of incredulity, concern, and sorrow simultaneously displayed on her face.

We talked late into the night. We read scripture after scripture about dreams, why God gives dreams, and the significance of that gift. Admittedly, my disposition was not suddenly and miraculously changed. That took some time. Nevertheless, I understood more truth about dreams and the wrongness of praying against how the Holy Spirit wanted to work in my life.

Wavering between excitement and fear, I returned home. I expected I would dream. I wanted the gift, but I must admit I still wanted it my way.

Over the next few weeks, I repented of my stubbornness and ignorance. Both had caused me to resent a precious gift of the Spirit and His operation. Oh, there were so many lessons I still needed to learn. God "who is rich in mercy" suddenly began to give me dreams again without my asking, but not before I repented for discounting and denying what He'd called me to do (Ephesians 2:4). As my dreams began to flow again, I still could not remember many, which troubled me, but I did not dwell on that part.

Even today, I continue to develop a personal culture of dreams. This culture is rooted in thankfulness, gratitude, and a deeper humility.

Get Ready

In 2014, I attended my first Global Awakening Conference. Through various teachings on words of knowledge, once again I felt affirmed in what I'd learned in my church as a little girl, that dreams were one context in which we could receive a word of knowledge. The conference built on the discussions I'd had with my mentor in Chattanooga. I was fascinated, amazed, and excited about any future dreams I might have. I believed I would be better able to receive and understand them. I resolved to stop cringing at what I perceived as a bad dream—the ones I'd classified as nightmares, the dreams about someone's death.

With the passage of four years, I found myself standing amidst the sea of eager faces once again at yet another Global Awakening conference, this time with a few folks from my church. The familiarity of the setting was no mere chance; rather, I perceived it was a testament to another meticulous thread of God's extraordinary plan being woven into my life.

As our group gathered, waiting for the shuttle that would return us to the comfort of our hotel, little did I know that this mundane moment would turn into a captivating event, witnessed not just by me but also by my dear friend Alyce as well.

Here's her account:

> I attended a Randy Clark School of Healing and
> Impartation sponsored by Bethel Church in Redding,
> California, in January of 2018, with a group from my

church. While there, Mari and I were outside the Redding Convention Center waiting for the shuttle back to our hotel. A man we did not know walked past us, stopped, and walked backward to get to Mari! He looked at her and said, "The Lord is going to increase your dreams and visions."

The gentleman's announcement was so startling that I could only manage a quiet "thank you."

I had said "yes" to dreams again, and God was already fully restoring my gift of visions and dreams. I pondered the timing of this prophecy the rest of the evening.

God, who knew me before I was formed in my mother's womb (Psalm 139:13), in His loving kindness had over the years prepared my heart so I could receive a prophetic word. That word would radically change my life and ministry. Even now, when I recall the incident, the gentleman's astounding words leave me wonderstruck.

The Increase

One week after I returned home, on January 28, 2018, I experienced the first of a multitude of vivid dreams. Since then, I've sometimes had as many as four or five dreams every night or morning.

Nearly five years later, God has blessed me with over two thousand dreams and visions. I find it astonishing, and yet even more incredible is the rapidity with which the dreams have come true. Many have come true immediately, others didn't come to pass for a few years, and I'm still waiting to see the rest fulfilled. And the revelations continue.

While I was writing this book, I heard these words in my heart, "I've anointed you to dream."

God has shaped, designed, and blessed my gift to dream. I have become keenly aware that this would be one way He would communicate, commune, and connect with me more deeply than He had before. More importantly, I know that even now He wants to increase my faith in hearing His voice and understanding His desire to unfold His rich secrets through dreams and visions to me.

I am excited and humbled.

You might think this is a great ending; however, my story doesn't conclude here. There is more to be learned.

Chapter 4: The Dreams

Dreams. Why do discussions about this topic always arouse such deep emotions in us? Varying talking points during a conversation with a dreamer are approached with curiosity, suspicion, admiration, or excitement. People rarely forget such conversations. Some leave inspired to pay closer attention to their dreams; others remain skeptical. At least, this has been my experience with those who believe in the validity of such dream experiences and those who do not.

This was never more apparent to me than the time I was teaching a workshop on gifts of the Spirit, specifically the word of knowledge, wisdom, and discernment of spirits. I mentioned how dreams could fit into the first category, and my comments and examples were met with enthusiasm, curiosity, and joy by some attendees. Others, though silent, were not in agreement. Those who vocalized their disagreement based it on the need for the gift of dreams in biblical times but believed it was no longer needed in contemporary Christianity.

Skeptics ridicule the belief that God divinely gives dreams, and sadly, even some of those committed to biblical inerrancy are skeptical. Biblical and secular scholars often struggle with understanding or explaining the purpose of a God-given dream or night vision in the 21st century.

However, dreams are elements of the deep mysteries of life and the unknown. Hence, there are a myriad of ideas about dreams, and in conversations I've been politely and abruptly introduced to different schools of thought on the subject. While I don't suggest these to all be formal schools of thought, for simplicity's sake I have listed a few ideologies as schools of thought.

School of Oneirologists

People who study the science of dreams are called oneirologists. They have tried to understand dreams by conducting multitudes of studies. However, they conclude dreams are as varied as individuals, and they are simply too complicated to categorize with certainty and specificity. Scientists and psychoanalysts offer no absolutes in explanations of what happens to cause our sleeping selves to dream. They conclude the dream has all to do with multi-layered, complicated underpinnings that are impossible to fully identify.

How interesting that the distinguished and illustrious psychologists Carl Jung and Sigmund Freud had a well-publicized and bitter disagreement over the theory of why we dream. So sore was their dispute that they ended their friendship.

As we transition from Jung and Freud's disagreement on dream interpretation, let's delve into the perspective of those who view dreaming as one of our body's natural responses. This brings us to the School of Natural Responses.

School of Natural Responses

This group believes that humans must dream because dreaming is one of our body's natural responses. They consider the dream state as the time we unconsciously sort through past and present unresolved conflicts or problems. This school of thought bases its premise on the idea that our dreams are the culmination of views concerning the stresses we experience during the day's events. Further, they believe that dreams are our brain's way of processing and problem-solving what we cannot handle during our waking hours.

I understand and agree there may be times when one processes life issues while asleep. However, I do not wholeheartedly ascribe to that ideology. My dream experiences have been about situations, circumstances, and people utterly unknown to me, and yet somehow their struggles, questions, or needs appear in my dreams. These dreams do not refer in any way to my personal conflict, past or present. I do not think I am unique in this regard. But to the point about processing something we're dealing within life, be that as it may, God is still the giver of that great dream.

Not All Dreams Are Serious

In 2021, a friend invited me to lunch as the world began to open back up for business after the global Covid-19 pandemic. We set the date for January 21st. I'd had a dream two weeks before, on January 7th.

> **Dream**
>
> My friend Amanda and I are seated side by side at a small café table. A waiter brings two bottles, one yellow and one pink Italian lemonade, and puts them in front of us with a grand gesture. I receive the yellow one; she receives the pink one.

We met for lunch at the appointed time, and my friend was seated across from me at a small table. The room was boisterous, and it was difficult for us to hear each other. She asked, "Do you mind if I come around and sit next to you?"

I told her, "Of course not. That's fine."

When the waiter came, he asked what we would like to drink. She said, "I'd like a glass of lemonade," and I decided to follow suit.

After he left, I smiled at my friend and told her that I had something to give her. Before meeting her, God led me to print out a copy of my dream, and after we both ordered our lemonades, I thought, now's the time to give it to her.

When I handed her the printout of the dream, at first, she was speechless, but then we both had a good laugh as we marveled at how the dream played out. How sweet of the Lord to give a dream about what would happen and how. God is wholly and completely in charge of our sleep time.

School of Randomness

Still, others believe our dreams are merely a result of random factors—what we've eaten, our conversations, and interactions with family members, coworkers, medical professionals, or strangers. They may also believe dreams result from influences from what we've read or watched on television and or in movies before sleeping.

School of Unbelief

With skepticism abounding, there is yet another perspective that presents a viewpoint which challenges even the notion of dreaming, as some remain resolute in their conviction that dreams are a realm beyond human experience.

Some do not believe anyone dreams at all. This attitude, however, is disputed by oneirologists. Scientists and psychologists state that dreaming is necessary. (See above.)

Others have concluded spiritually significant dreams ceased centuries ago after John wrote the book of Revelation. Generally, this is a position many Cessationists hold today: dreams have no place in the 21st century. [1]

As I consider the various schools of thought (excluding the School of Unbelief), it becomes evident that while each have some merit and to a certain extent some truth, each school of thought has, in my opinion, significant holes in their theories.

School of Mari

I believe there is only one answer as to why we dream. Dreams are given to us by God for His purposes. His desire to reveal His secrets through dreams is to bless, warn, encourage, instruct, and inspire us. We know this because He continuously pours out from His heart of love. Dreams give us a new appreciation for His character: love, mercy, goodness, and grace.

In the midst of all the examinations, discussions, ideologies, and theories, one truth remains unwavering: God stands as the ultimate authority. His steadfast message is profound in its simplicity.

Here's what God as the final authority says about dreams:

> For God speaks again and again,
> though people do not recognize it.
> He speaks in dreams, in visions of the night,
> when deep sleep falls on people
> as they lie in their beds.
> He whispers in their ears
> and terrifies them with warnings.
> Job 33:14-8 (NLT)

God Gives Us Dreams

If indeed dreams do come from God, you might ask, "What about nightmares?"

Consider Job 33:18, just quoted. Sometimes dreams from God terrify us. Is it possible that nightmares result from demonic forces that have acquired full charge of our dreams? There certainly could be, on the rare occasion, satanic influences *attempting* to initiate fear and intimidation while we sleep.

Most assuredly, the presence of God is more significant in us, even while we sleep, than any disruptive message Satan tries to communicate. Hence, what would be considered a nightmare is in actuality a spiritual battle. In which case, we are always victorious by the end of the dream, and through the interpretation. I hope you will see evidence of this as you read the dreams I present throughout the book.

The average person, it is said, dreams approximately three to seven times during the night, but the dreams are immediately forgotten and lost to memory. I am blessed in that I remember at least ninety percent of the dreams I know I had. Often, the memory of the dream fades within the first few seconds after waking up, so no matter how groggy I feel, I keep an account of my dreams by speaking into a recorder or writing in a notepad I keep at my bedside. The secret is discipline—to wake up after the dream and capture as much of it as possible. In all honesty, sometimes sleep wins out. I understand, though, based on this statistic of not remembering all our dreams, it's possible that when I wake up, sometimes I don't even know I had one.

Biblical Examples of Dreams

To say that dreams are a mystery is an understatement. Throughout Scripture, we read how God used dreams to convert hearts, give hope, rescue, direct steps, save lives, and save nations. He often gave more than one dream to the same person with a similar message. Many of us have heard their stories:

> Abimelech: "But God came to Abimelech in a dream by night, and said to him, 'Indeed you are a dead man because of the woman whom you have taken, for she is a man's wife.'" (Genesis 20:3 NKJV)

The Three Kings: "Then, being divinely warned in a dream that they should not return to Herod, they departed for their own country another way." (Matthew 2:12 NKJV)

Each of these dreams was a prophetic warning and came to pass.

Many stories and testimonies recorded in the New Testament—particularly in the Gospel of Matthew, called a book of dreams, along with the books of Acts, 2 Corinthians, and Revelation—confirm that God did not stop giving dreams in the Old Testament. How interesting that the Scriptures end with an incredible and crucial vision of future world events.

God's approach to communication through dreams is multifarious. In other words, it is varied to the extent that it would be challenging to keep a tally of how many ways He can give us a dream. God is fully creative enough—nay, *more than able*—to speak, show, alert, or warn us in numerous ways. This is a fact too complex for the human mind to grasp. It is impossible for our God to ever run out of ingenious visualizations. He is always able to make Himself and His divine will known to us in unfathomable mysteries as we sleep.

I have had a few recurring dreams for years, with the same scene or person appearing. To the best of my understanding, these repetitive dreams may help me learn additional principles or words of knowledge. Once I understood the principle or the truth God wanted to reveal through His Holy Spirit, I never had the dream again. That is a spiritual victory.

If God worked through dreams in the Old and New Testaments, we reap the blessings of every scriptural promise to us about receiving dreams from God.

If you want to dream more, let me encourage you to consider asking God to speak to you through dreams. Reflect on your dreams, pray about their potential meanings, and pray for someone to help you with a godly interpretation.

Chapter 5: The Gift

Scripture informs us that God apportions our gifts to strengthen the body of Christ and for our eternal benefit:

Having then gifts differing according to the grace that is given to us,
whether prophecy, *let us prophesy* according to the proportion of faith.
Romans 12:6 (KJV)

One of the many ways God shows love for us and connects to humans is through dreams and visions. Although I lived closely with the Lord and loved Him deeply, I intentionally tried to sever the dream connection. As I mentioned previously, my spiritual immaturity led me to believe dreaming was a gift I could live without.

Today, it is hard to imagine there was ever a time when I did not want to steward the gift God had specially and specifically designed for my life on earth. As Psalm 139:14 says, "I am fearfully and wonderfully made" (KJV). Part of God's design for me was the gift of dreams.

We do not choose our initial spiritual gifts (1 Corinthians 12:4, 8–11, 14:1). Nor do we choose how they will operate. But we can be thankful for them, trust them, and rely on the Holy Spirit's wisdom in giving them to us. We are to be faithful with what we receive, plus desire and ask for more of that gift and other gifts. Had I understood this principle sooner, I would have been farther along on this dream journey.

God is incredibly generous with His gifts; we are considerably more gifted and creative than we realize. Sometimes, though, Satan deceives us into thinking otherwise. However, in the spirit realm, we have a greater capacity for receiving spiritual gifts than many Christians will venture forth to accept because of fear, poor spiritual education, prejudices, or unbelief about spiritual gifts, and so on.

Prophecy is mentioned more than any other gift in the New Testament, and dreams are one of the ways God entrusts or reveals prophetic information to us. While the gift of prophecy may manifest in many ways beyond our capacity to name or explain, I hope that none would dispute that it is one of the primary ways in which dreams as divine revelation come. Prophecy may involve the future, as in years from now, or it may be something that will happen within hours, days, weeks, or months from the time of the dream.

Prophetic Visions

To broaden this discussion, I would like to include the subject of visions, for visions are most definitely prophetic.

It is paramount to understand that all visions are not from God. Scripture is clear. Some are from an individual's vain imaginings, and others are demonic. (See Romans 12:6; 1 Corinthians 12:28–29.)

We must understand the necessity of discerning the origins of a dream or vision. How do you discern truth from lies?

1. Pray and ask God to give you a complete understanding of the vision you have seen.
2. Judge the vision. False visions lead people away from God's will. In Matthew 4:8, we find a startling passage: Satan gave Jesus Himself a vision of all the world's kingdoms. We know the outcome. If Satan can give false

visions to Jesus, of all people, his demonic tormentors can show one to us.

3. Always place a vision against the Word to see if it matches God's purposes and will. Never allow pride to cause you to make a vision fit Scripture.

4. Ask for another's opinion on the interpretation.

Prophetic visions and dreams can reveal God's heart for specific individuals, the church, the nation, or a larger world context. In any case, no one—apart from God—knows what will take place in the future.

When you are a dreamer, this gift of the prophetic is both humbling and fearsome. It is humbling because it is ever apparent that we did nothing that deserved or warranted the gift, and it is fearsome because we have seen something God has shown us only. We are responsible for some sacred secret or holy insight He has revealed, and we must pray it back to Him to know what He intends for us to do—or not do—with the information. Whether the dreams seem to carry the theme of death, as so many of mine did in the earlier years, or complex messages for loved ones, friends, or the church, if you are a dreamer, receive your dream with thankfulness, not dread, for you are not cursed with the gift of dreaming, you are blessed.

The Red Jeep Dream

On December 7, 2021, I stood in the doorway of an auto body shop looking at a red Jeep. I saw the Jeep with its hood up, and the two front doors were open.

Three days later, December 10, 2021, the accident occurred. One of my children had a car accident because of running a stop sign they didn't see. Fortunately, they were driving under 30 mph, but they were afraid the vehicle was totaled. The Jeep had to be towed to the dealership. I was able to offer encouragement that the car could be repaired. It would just need some work.

Chapter 6: The Talk

Early on, I shared my dreams with friends and family, though I lacked deep understanding or wisdom. I was cautious, choosing to share only the dreams I perceived as positive or those with blessings. Eventually, boldness became my driving force. I looked for the person I had dreamed about, or I phoned them and blurted out that I had a dream. "Here is what happened," I said, and that was it. I just told the dream to whoever was in it. I was overzealous.

Occasionally, the Holy Spirit gave me an interpretation. However, I wasn't deterred if He didn't. I often shared the dream even if I didn't fully comprehend it, leaving the interpretation to the listener's discretion. In hindsight, this was not the wisest approach. I did not pray or consult God before talking about my dream. I did not fully understand the Holy Spirit has a time and opportunity in mind for when to share a dream or if it is to be shared.

Many years have passed, and I have acquired more understanding and knowledge about God, dreams, and their telling.

Follow God's Direction

Have you ever told a dream out of time? Timing is everything when relating a dream to someone. Here's what I've learned: follow God's timing in telling the dream. Let God direct the telling. Ask Him if or when He wants you to share the dream. Ask the Lord to give you an opening during a conversation with the person you want to tell. Pray for that person to bring up a topic that will become a natural segue into a discussion about your dream.

It's always best to seek an understanding of the Lord's purpose behind the dream. Although it may not be apparent to the hearer, the interpretation may be more understandable than the dream itself, which may be all He intends for you to share. At other times, God may give you an urgency, a nudge in your spirit, meaning speak it now, make haste to tell the dream.

Since He is the one who gave us the dream, so He is also the one to lead us in when and where we share what He wants us to know. It may not always be His plan for the entire dream to be revealed. He knows what He wants to accomplish; we do not see it as He does. We must trust Him in that.

Ultimately, it comes down to entrusting both the dream and its interpretation to the Holy Spirit, relinquishing any desire for personal control. We give God all the glory and honor this way. After all, the dream and the interpretation never belonged to us. This is always the correct response.

Understanding this principle determines whether we make spiritual progress. To disregard it will retard our spiritual growth in this area.

The recipient of the dream interpretation has a role to play as well. Those who believed God communicated through my dreams took action based on them, be it for encouragement, warnings, creative inspiration, or even a business idea.

Every dream we have is not necessarily one we will ever divulge to others. I have dreams a few decades old that I have never shared, but I have still witnessed the dream fulfilled. Why didn't I share it? Because I wasn't instructed to. Sometimes God may give us a dream about others so we can pray about their plight, life circumstances, deliverance, salvation, etc. In many instances, I've had dreams about people I didn't know very well, if at all, or a situation that was strange to me. I knew, or rather have learned, that it means to pray without ceasing. Dreams will build your prayer life.

The following dream is an example of this principle.

The Train Dream

I am on a train. There is also another woman on it, and we are talking. She has been traveling longer than I have. I get off when I reach my destination, and she does too. We continue our conversation. I see police or uniformed guards looking for a young man to arrest him. They have prevented the train from leaving and have begun searching. The woman is concerned and does not want them to find him. I feel as though she is trying to protect him. Then they find a body. Someone has been shot. They find another body; this one has been lynched, another hanged. A fourth young man has drowned. Five or six bodies lie in a row on the ground. The police or guards still cannot find the person they seek. As the onlooker in the dream, I am horrified that these people were killed just to find one particular man.

This dream was obviously about death. The morning after the dream, I received a call from someone telling me about a mutual friend's son who had died suddenly. The following day, I received a call from another friend to tell me her father-in-law had died from a heart attack. The next day, a call came for me to pray as a family looked for their three-year-old son. They discovered he'd drowned two days later. The following week, I received news of another death, a family whose son had overdosed. Four deaths. The reports had me reeling.

Interpretation: Dixie

Mari's dream points to a call for prayer, asking for God's mercy upon the fifth man, that he might have time to repent and find his purpose in life and ministry in Christ. In John 10:10 Jesus said, "The thief comes only to steal, kill, and destroy. I came that they may have life and have it abundantly" (ESV).

I didn't know the missing man's identity, but I prayed anyway. Later on, I received divine insight, a word from the Lord, which unveiled the identity of the man. I immediately contacted his mother, a dear friend from my church. I told her I wanted to share a dream, and she was very receptive. As it turned out, her son had been in a car accident the week of the four tragedies. The following week, he was in a second near-fatal car accident. His mother and I agreed he was the fifth person in the dream. The fervent prayers of many formed a shield of protection around him. I was happy to learn he is getting his life back on track.

Chapter 7: The Skeptics

Have you ever told a dream to someone, and the listener initially disagreed with or disbelieved what you said and refused to act on your warning or urgings? Perhaps Pilate's wife experienced this as she fearfully yet urgently adjured her husband to have nothing to do with Jesus, whom she described as "that just man" (KJV).

> "'Have nothing to do with that righteous *and* innocent Man;
> for last night I suffered greatly in a dream because of Him.'"
> Matthew 27:19 (AMP)

Thankfully, Pilate listened to her warning.

Here is one truth to consider: Among the many people God has gifted to the body of Christ, our collective growth is hindered if we remain confined by traditional religious belief systems. These systems often breed skepticism toward dreamers and their dreams. It is true there are, and have always been, people who present themselves as dreamers but, unfortunately, are nothing more than wolves in sheep's clothing, preying on the unsuspecting, undiscerning Christian. Yet despite our doubts, God reveals His divine purpose, plan, and will through visions or dreams, inspiring both the dreamer and those who hear the dream. Our omniscient

God and His choice of revealing mysteries cannot be unfolded and placed in boxes and labels of our doctrinal preferences.

Don't Take It Personally

Thankfully, the skepticism of those who are unbelieving, unconvinced, unimpressed, and unwilling to accept my dream about them no longer stops me from sharing a dream when I feel led to do so.

I stopped taking the negativism personally. As I stated earlier, release the responsibility of the dream. These dreams are God's messages. He is responsible for the outcome.

As a dreamer, exercise caution in how you handle the gift in the form of a word of knowledge and prophecy. A person's willingness or unwillingness to hear a dream and the interpretation will depend on their level of spiritual maturity. Mature believers are not afraid to trust God. Their ability to receive depends on the depth of their relationship with the Lord. They will know automatically to listen and then pray to God concerning what they've heard. they will also be better at discerning when dreams are *not* from God.

Your ministry as a dreamer should be devoid of hypersensitivity or an inflated ego. You cannot impose your dreams on others forcefully—that is, beat them over the head. However, you cannot afford to doubt your dreams, nor should you allow others to make you doubt them. I've experienced that more than a few times.

People have spoken to me with straight, serious faces, denying the truth or relevance of a dream or an interpretation I shared with them. Those with whom I hold close relationships posed more of a challenge. Before I better understood what God was doing, anyone who became defensive or took offense at something I shared would cause me to shut down. In my desire to avoid conflict, I immediately deferred to their disbelief and discounted what I had dreamed. I avoided a disagreement at all costs, no matter how convinced I was that the dream was truth.

Cultivate a Tender Heart

In general, someone walking in the light values God-given dreams. However, consider a scenario where I dreamed about a woman whom we'll refer to as Jane. In the dream, God reveals she has a secret sin. If left unconfessed, this sin will destroy her in many ways: spiritually, her reputation or career; or physically, through sickness or disease. If the Lord directs, "Tell Jane the dream," it will be because He has already given her the opportunity to repent, and she has ignored His voice.

We see this principle in Daniel 4:27–31 with King Nebuchadnezzar. He had a disturbing dream, and God gave Daniel the interpretation, which was a warning to the king about being exalted in his mind.

The Lord only exposes us if we are unwilling to heed what He says the first time. We will need no further warning if we respond positively rather than hardening our hearts (see Hebrews 3:7–8 and Psalm 95:7–8). We gladly want His help or insight in any way He sends it. But King Nebuchadnezzar ignored God's words, and the dream came to pass.

Another example illustrating the extent of people's skepticism toward dreams takes this further. Let's say Jane not only refuses to discern if the Lord may be revealing something to her, but she also turns against the dreamer—rebuking, rebuffing, shunning, or accusing the dreamer of fishing around for information under the guise of relating a dream.

Unfortunately, this is a familiar scenario and can be especially true when leaders are approached with a dream. They may feel insecure and insist they alone have a direct line to God. He would never need to send someone else to give them a word of knowledge. Sadly, I have seen this play out time and again.

Years ago, I dreamed about a man planning to leave the pastorate. He had decided to pursue a different career path and intended to depart without informing the congregation. He and his wife had yet to finish formulating their plans. She was shocked when I mentioned a dream about their plans.

Soon after, I went to the church for a meeting. The session focused on this minister's determination to discover who had leaked his plans to me. He wanted to deal with the disloyal staff member and tried to intimidate me into divulging who it was. I could only direct him to the Holy Spirit—time and again.

His facial expression reflected calm and control as I spoke, but I discerned the man was shaken. I also realized he knew I was a dreamer, and though it galled him, he had no choice but to believe the dream and quickly dismissed me from the meeting.

God Can Surprise Us

I also dreamed about a young mom who was pregnant with a little boy. When I shared this dream with her mother—a dear friend—she plainly told me that her daughter and son-in-law weren't planning to have any more children. They already had two little girls, and she insisted they were pretty satisfied that two were enough. She then gave me a few more insights on how improbable the dream was, so I held my peace. Two years later, this friend called to announce her daughter's pregnancy and that they had discovered it was a boy!

"Congratulations! I'm not at all surprised," I responded. "Remember, I dreamed about it?"

On another occasion, I was passionately discussing dreams with a friend. I mentioned a recent dream I had about her. I'll always remember her response.

"I don't believe in dreams; dreams are not for today."

I was taken aback! I knew she was a follower of Christ who believed in the scriptures. After all, aren't dreams mentioned in the scriptures?

I asked her if I could share the dream, and she agreed. In the dream, she was wearing a white lab coat and stood at the front of a room, seemingly teaching. I felt a bit embarrassed and let the conversation fade because she laughed!

A few months later, a homeschool group the woman and I were both part of decided to offer a variety of classes through a homeschool co-op for students. As leaders, we each were required to teach at least one class. On one occasion, I finished my class session earlier than usual and decided to sit in on the class my children were attending. I slipped into a seat in the back of this friend's classroom and had to suppress a giggle.

She stood in the front of the room teaching biology, wearing a white lab coat! When she dismissed the students and gathered her things, I gently reminded her of my long-ago dream and the classroom setting we were now standing in.

It was her turn to be stunned.

How wonderful to learn years later that she became a believer in God-given dreams.

Access the Phenomenal

Drawing someone's focus back to a dream isn't about bragging; it's about illuminating the truth of the dream to bring glory to God.

Imagine if a person's belief system and theology restricted God to actions only described in commentaries or in the Bible—like parting the Red Sea, feeding the five thousand, and healing ten lepers. Such limitations stifle the possibility of envisioning God performing even more extraordinary deeds through us or others.

On the contrary, if someone's belief system and theology don't confine God's miraculous work within biblical parameters—scriptural accounts of the miracles only and no others can exist outside of what they've read—they won't dismiss passages like Ephesians 3:20 (NIV):

Now to him who is able to do immeasurably more than all we ask or imagine,
according to his power that is at work within us,
to him be glory in the church and in Christ Jesus
throughout all generations, for ever and ever! Amen.

Also, consider "Is anything too hard for the LORD?" (Genesis 18:14 NKJV).

In this case, they will be open to receiving dreams and visions, and asking God for more.

Dreams of the Spirit come in diverse forms. Even when dreams share repetitive themes, they offer various lessons. His faithfulness is evident in this. The dreams He gives are new every morning, just like His mercies (Lamentations 3:23).

Dream

Mari as an Overdressed Counselor

I am talking to someone, counseling them in quiet tones. At the same time, I am observing myself. The one I am counseling faces me, the speaker. As the observer, I only see the back of myself.

I am wearing a royal blue dress with a flared skirt, sleeveless—very dressy.

As the observer, I wonder why I am all dressed up for such an ordinary situation.

Interpretation: Dixie

This dream is a commendation and represents an extraordinary occasion from heaven's point of view. The person being counseled trusts you to help and desires what the Lord will say through you. This person may have been praying for this answer; therefore, what you speak will be the answer needed. Being a counselor is the Lord's kingdom work; it is an honor and a great responsibility as well. You bring your best to the situation.

Chapter 8: The Keys

The concept of God's will being done on earth as it is in heaven should apply to every divine dream. One evening, I found myself in fervent prayer over a persistent and challenging situation that had lingered far too long in the life of one of my adult children. During this earnest moment, I experienced the gentle voice of the Holy Spirit speaking to me, conveying a profound truth: "Your dreams are the answer to your prayers."

The dreams I had received contained intricate details and specific insights into the decisions and circumstances of my child. You can well imagine the elation that surged within me upon receiving this revelation. Naturally, I longed for these dreams to promptly materialize, seeking an immediate realization. The desire for resolution was strong, almost impatient. I wanted the prayer answered yesterday! But rather than instant fulfillment, this revelation brought to light my need for patience and unwavering trust.

Upon revisiting these dreams and carefully considering their sequence, a compelling narrative emerged—a story woven with God's faithful promises to me. The story unfolded with themes of deliverance, repentance, and restoration, gracefully entwined within each interpretation. This journey of dreams and interpretations was, in itself, a testament to the building of one's faith. It became increasingly evident that if the dreams concerning not only myself but also others had come to pass, then undoubtedly, those regarding my children would be no different.

Dreams, I came to understand, are glimpses of reality as it exists in heaven; they embody the divine will of the Father. God's plans for each individual—whether man, woman, or child—are already known to Him (Jeremiah 29:11). Our task lies in aligning our spirit with His divine will, harmonizing our desires with heaven's dream. In essence, we strive to possess the mind of Christ. This realization fuels our prayers for the fulfillment of the dream's interpretation, for the realization of God's purpose on earth. And here, in this very point, lies my greatest excitement.

A dream that imparts a warning serves as a call to action—an urging to repent or to intercede on behalf of another. Conversely, a dream interpreted as a promise becomes a catalyst for our prayers, stirring us to seek deeper insights, revelations, healing, prosperity, wisdom, or knowledge.

Dream

I am standing by a window in my bedroom. I hear an enormous clap of thunder which shakes the house.

Interpretation: Dixie

Spiritually, thunder occurs when two totally different, very strong climates or attitudes or people collide, as in nature when hot and cold fronts are on a collision course. The climates, attitudes, or people will hover over you, strong and reverberating through your house, life, or in your church. Either way, although this thunder is loud and gets your attention, it does not seem to damage you, even though it rattles the windows and shakes the house.

Through the lens of faith, we begin to perceive what God desires in heaven and will bring to fruition here on earth, all through the conduit of our earnest prayers.

Chapter 9: The Dreamer

God has anointed me to dream. It is not an earned honor, but one granted by grace alone.

As I teach workshops or speak with individuals, I try to reveal the truth about dreams relative to the character of God and what He is trying to convey to us as we sleep. It is always about His lovingkindness, mercy, and grace toward us.

Consider how a loving parent, taking his young child for a walk, is aware the child will one day walk down the street alone. The parent's love points out the beauty of their surroundings but also compels the parent to make the child keenly aware of problems, perils, and pitfalls. Our heavenly Father's love and concern for us exceeds that of any earthly parents. As our loving Father, the difficult or complex dreams He gives us may conceal the blessings, treasures, or successes He has for us. What I thought were unpleasant dreams contained precious truths, deeply hidden in the frightening presentation of the so-called bad dream. I now honor God for all the dreams He has given me from childhood until now.

What a joy to share my dreams and interpretations with family and friends and watch them make conscientious, God-directed decisions or approach life with a new joy or confidence on the path they were already walking. I have seen many ministries birthed or blossom. My dreams have frightened, troubled, and sometimes even angered the recipient, but my dreams have also encouraged, affirmed, and blessed others.

Sharing the Dream

Whenever people respond angrily, coolly, or make jokes or use sarcasm when I mention I have had a dream about them, it is usually for one of a few reasons:

- **First, they may be offended** that God would give someone else a dream about them rather than speak to them directly. Almost certainly, they will disregard the dream or vision. It will not be regarded as authentic because it did not come as they believed it should.

- **Second, they may believe they are the spiritual superior** or on the same **spiritual peer level** as the dreamer, and it is exceedingly difficult for them to accept the dream and interpretation. The messenger is more the problem than the dream itself.

- **Third, they believe it is improbable God gives anyone a dream or vision.** Non-Christians—and unfortunately, some Christians—fall into this category. It is easier to mock or joke about things not easily understood. It is hard for them to imagine God using Old and New Testament ways in the 21st century. But in Ephesians 3:20, the apostle Paul encourages us to recognize that God will go beyond our wildest imaginings if we have the faith to believe in Him.

The good news is that every dream from God comes to pass sooner or later, with or without other people's approval.

The Dream Team

Fortunately, there have been many more times when people were delighted by the dream and the interpretation. It gave them hope for the promises of God as a result of the message of the dream or how the interpretation always brought glory to God.

What a blessing to share with those who open their hearts to hearing what the Lord has for them when He speaks through dreams. How wonderful it is when the dreamer, the interpreter, and the recipient praise God for what He has shown them. When this is the case, all three can share in the learning journey. As they listen, they will gain more understanding as the fullness of the dream opens to them. In the end, the results are for the furtherance of kingdom work.

One night, as I lay down to sleep, I boldly asked for a dream, and God answered me with not just one but several dreams.

Sometimes, I've asked Him to give me a dream specifically about something He knew would happen the next day, and occasionally, He has. Night or morning, whenever I ask, I dream. I encourage you to exercise your faith in receiving dreams; God will hear and answer. He loves faith.

I am grateful and encouraged that my experiences and audiences have flourished over the past several years. Friends and strangers continue to contact me to tell me the dreams they've had, to ask questions, or to have their dreams interpreted. Two of my adult children are starting to dream more often, and they call to share their dream and wait with faithful expectation for the interpretation. It is an exciting season in my life and ministry, and I am learning from the best teachers—the Holy Spirit and my mentor.

As you turn the pages of this book, I hope that you are inspired to go beyond the comfortable and familiar by asking for more dreams and that your expectation of the work of the Holy Spirit in your life will continue to develop in this area. He is willing, are you?

Dream

I am headed to a workshop or class. I am a little late because I can't find the classroom. As I hurry through the maze-like corridors of the unfamiliar building, my footsteps echoing in the empty hallways, I can't shake the feeling of being lost in a labyrinth. When I enter the right room, the instructor has already started the lecture. I sit by some friends who are going through boxes with compartments. They tell me one has a lot of silverware, especially forks, in it. I don't have silverware, so this is an excellent opportunity to obtain some, since it is free. I start to gather some.

Interpretation: Dixie

Some people will provide directions to find things you don't have but need. It won't cost a cent. What you find will enhance the spiritual dining experience you want and the substantial meat of the Word you want to provide for others.

Chapter 10: The Interpretation

I have someone who regularly interprets my dreams. What an honor it is. I cannot emphasize the value and importance of trusting your dreams to someone who receives God-given interpretations.

The only way for a spiritual dream to have a spiritual interpretation and biblical soundness is for the interpreter to be Spirit-filled, biblically sound, and have the gift of wisdom operating in their life daily. Indeed, I've been blessed to have such a person in my life.

An internet search will yield thousands of results for just about any project you want to build or make, with step-by-step instructions. Dream interpretation is not a DIY (Do It Yourself) project; watching someone and mimicking their response or actions will never yield sought-after results. Dream interpretation is dependent on what the Holy Spirit says a dream means.

We can try to interpret our dreams, yet God wants us to ask for the gift of interpretation, and while He is teaching us about it, He will be expanding that gift in us. However, it is wise to have someone listen to whatever interpretation we may receive to see if God has more to add. We should be willing to rely on God to provide an interpreter to help discern the message sent. It should never be a problem to interpret your dream and offer it back to God but also submit it to someone else who may have a more substantial gift of interpretation and see if what you interpret is confirmed.

Some dreamers insist on absolute control over their dreams. Once an interpretation is known, it is no longer under the jurisdiction of the interpreter. Feel free to ask for confirmation or another opinion of dream interpretation. I've seen instances where people would rather not ask about confirmation for a dream because they are stuck on being the one to interpret it.

I don't believe that's how the body of Christ operates. Humility allows us to ask someone else to hear from God for us. It's too easy for a spirit of pride to creep in, otherwise. Dixie McClintock has the gift of wisdom and dream interpretation. God brought us together many years ago, first as a mentor (Dixie) and mentee (me). Over the years, our relationship developed into a deep friendship. I have her to thank for understanding what dreams are about, i.e., words of knowledge, God's messages to us, and the meaning of the messages. Dixie's ability to interpret dreams has increased exponentially since I began this dream adventure.

Interpretation of Dreams

Occasionally, when I mention how much I value Dixie's part in interpreting my dreams, a few friends or acquaintances will tell me —in a somewhat high-handed manner—that they interpret their own dreams. I congratulate them because I'm not offended. However, I encourage them to go beyond the first impressions of their interpretation. Don't get me wrong, interpreting your dreams is an excellent and desirable gift, but I ask them to bear these considerations in mind.

1. How many dreams do we read about in the Bible where there was no call for an interpreter? I usually get a blank stare when I ask this question. The answer is zero unless the dream was literal and no interpretation was needed. For example: "An angel of the Lord appeared to Joseph in a dream. 'Get up,' he said, 'take the child and his mother and escape to Egypt stay there until I tell you, for Herod is going to search for the child to kill him.' So he got up took the child and his mother during the night and left for Egypt" (Matthew 2:13 NIV). But in every other case, an interpretation was needed. In the Old Testament, Jacob's son, Joseph, was known as the interpreter of dreams and, in

turn, made the true and living God's name known among the heathen (Genesis 40:8).

2. Why settle for partial understanding when the entirety of God's message is available to us? It's been my experience that when I interpret my dreams and share both dreams and interpretations with Dixie, the Lord nearly always adds more to them. In other words, a dreamer may have a basic understanding of a dream, but with the help or ministry of a woman or man of God, the Holy Spirit can reveal so much more.

3. Could confirmation of your dream come from sharing your interpretation and seeing if it's on point with the message the Lord wants you to receive? Absolutely, because, yes, sometimes we just don't get it right all by ourselves, and this is where the body of Christ comes in. We help one another. Sharing the interpretation opens the full blessing of the dream's meaning. Don't shy away from the opportunity to confirm your interpretation. By all means, don't let reluctance to share your interpretation result from pride or embarrassment—not wanting anyone else to know a particular lesson (personal sin or shortcoming) a dream has revealed. In any case, the Holy Spirit is more than able to consistently give you someone to partner with you in your

gift of dreams. It goes without saying that person also becomes a confidant.

I've asked Dixie to share her knowledge about interpreting dreams and what God has taught her about unlocking His secrets. Let's delve into the insights of someone who possesses the gift of wisdom and dream interpretation.

Dixie's Perspective on Interpretation

The ability to interpret or translate a symbolic dream into the message it contains is a gift from the Lord. Dream interpretation falls within the broader category of prophetic gifts and more specifically align with the spiritual gifts of "word of knowledge" and "word of wisdom" (1 Corinthians 12:8).

Interpretation of dreams is the work of the Holy Spirit, who shows the believer things to come (John 16:13). The interpretation is a personal message to His beloved child and sometimes applies to a broader audience if it is meant to be shared.

Dreams and their interpretations are not new to me. My brother, Scott, and I had received a prophecy that we would each inherit spiritually from our mother: dreams, visions, and teaching gifts. Our mother was experiencing dementia from brain damage caused by a high, long-lasting fever. (There was nothing wrong in her spirit, just her body and mind.) We asked her to bless us. For this to happen, we prayed that she could speak from her right mind so we could receive the legacy she wanted us to have. The Lord answered our prayer. Mother blessed us with those spiritual inheritances in clear, concise words.

In 2006, a friend told me the Lord had given her a message concerning me: "You are to be the interpreter of my dreams and visions," she said, "to help me understand the deeper meanings." Just as she said, this has happened over the years.

In 2017, a friend, Larry M., was in the hospital, and I was sitting with him while his wife went home for a few hours of rest. During our conversation, his pastor came in. After he prayed with Larry, he turned to me, a stranger, and said, "The Lord is giving you a more profound anointing. He's also giving you keys and gems of revelation." When I shared this story with a friend, she told me, "Keys unlock hidden things, gems, and treasures. It will be knowledge given and a realization that brings freedom."

Let's remember how I started interpreting dreams: Now and then, Mari would have a dream during her visits, and as she told me about it, I received the interpretation. Soon, she started having many dreams and continued to ask me to interpret for her. At first, if I was stuck, being insecure about this gift, I turned to Scott for help, but I became increasingly uneasy each time I called him. I believe the Lord was nudging me to have faith in Him, not in my brother.

It is now 2024, and the Lord has been faithful to Mari and me in giving us His messages in nearly two thousand dreams.

Dixie's Principles of Interpretation

The interpreter must have solid faith in God. The interpreter must know that the gift is God's wisdom. His purpose establishes it's anointed operation. The message is God's personal Word and revelation to the dreamer (and sometimes the interpreter). Doubts dishonor His desire to bring knowledge and understanding to the interpreter. The interpreter's faith must be in God and God alone.

Faith and love are essential. Both are the spiritual environment for the operation of the gift of Interpretation, given by Jesus Christ and empowered by the Holy Spirit:

Having then gifts differing according to the grace that is given to us, … *let us prophesy* according to the proportion of faith. (Romans 12:6 KJV)

And though I have *the gift of* prophecy, and understand all mysteries and all knowledge; and though I have all faith, so that I could remove mountains, but have not love, I am nothing. (1 Corinthians 13:2 NKJV)

Gifts cannot operate in faith alone; love is imperative. Without these two, the interpreter will interpret out of self-effort, not the Spirit.

Waiting is a part of faith. Sometimes interpretations have been immediate: as quickly as Mari telling me her dream and I knew what it meant. Yet more often than not, I had to wait a day or two, sometimes as much as a week, before I received an interpretation. While the Lord was teaching Mari about her anointing to dream, He was teaching me to rest in Him and wait patiently *with confidence* for His timing and revelation. He knew that too many immediate interpretations would harm my soul by inflating my ego. Since He had given her the dream as a message, He certainly would provide me with understanding. As I waited, I read Mari's dream(s) frequently and opened my heart to the Holy Spirit's guidance.

Think about it. There is so much in the Bible about people of faith waiting on God's revelations and His "due season" fulfillment: Joseph waited thirteen years to get out of prison in Egypt and much longer to see his dreams fulfilled (Genesis 37–50).

Learning to wait upon the Lord is vital to the Christian's spiritual development, which holds true in dream interpretation. Let me caution you not to rush ahead of the Holy Spirit and fall into the trap of calling something an interpretation that He has not given you.

If you can't get an interpretation, put the dream aside. Continue daily to believe for it, knowing the timing is up to the Lord, and thank Him in advance for what He will reveal "in due season." (Luke 12:2, Matthew 10:26) Remind yourself the Lord wants you to know the message of the dream and that you will receive it. Faith is where interpretation begins.

The Dreamer Can Also Interpret

Do Dixie's insights prompt you to think about a dream you've had? Do you see how the role of faith and love will work in your life? Let me, Mari, conclude by adding that sometimes the dreamer is also the interpreter. I've been able to interpret my dreams on a few occasions, and Dixie has confirmed the interpretations. However, most of the time, He has given me the dream and Dixie the interpretation to unite us with Him and each other in this ministry (Ephesians 4:12–15; 1 Corinthians 12:18–25, 14:26).

Dream

I am all set to tighten my daughter's braids. Our usual routine is me on the sofa, her on the floor. I decide to start with the right side. But as I gently turn her head, my fingers stumble upon a surprise—a bald spot, the size of a silver dollar. My bewilderment can't be concealed as I blurt out, "What happened to your hair?"

Interpretation: Dixie

You are to pray that this baldness goes away and is replaced with new covering. Also pray that your daughter sees quickly that decisions made without the Lord's directions and without consulting your spiritual wisdom from God are folly and will not result in any good outcome. Accepting that will be the start of new growth for her.

This dream was fulfilled the following day. I told my daughter about it, and she realized she needed my advice to help her solve a dilemma concerning a financial decision she had to make for her job. We were both glad she listened to the dream and chose to take my advice.

My daughter Rooney writes: "My mother's dreams have been a constant in my life. Rarely did a day go by when she wasn't telling us about a new one. Every once in a while, there'd be one about me, and though I'm a bit of a skeptic, it is hard to argue with accuracy!"

Dream

I am talking to my friend Chris. She says, "I am so happy you called because I had a dream about you." I ask her to tell me. She dreamed she was a fish swimming in a big sea. I tell her it is a good dream. Water can mean new birth, and involvement in evangelism. When I awake from the dream, I feel that I may have given her the wrong word. I think about Jesus making us fishers of men, but then Paul became all things to all men, so Chris may be a fish to be able to relate to other fish. I am unsure about my interpretation.

Interpretation: Dixie

This dream is not about your interpretation of it, which was correct. The two thoughts did not contradict. However, your feeling of uncertainty is the problem. The Lord is reminding you that a dream is His message to a person; therefore, He is the one responsible for ensuring it is delivered correctly. You feel it is your responsibility. He wants you to know He is the one who will give you the correct interpretation. You needn't worry; instead, relax in Him, knowing if you will just listen, you will receive the correct message. This is about you resting in Him, trusting Him in this new ministry of dream interpretation that He is giving you. He wouldn't give the dream to you if He didn't intend to provide the interpretation for it. See this as a blessing and as an honor to serve Him and others in this new spiritual gift.

Chapter 11: Types of Dreams

In the Old Testament, *ḥălôm* means *dream,* and in the New
Testament, *ónar* refers specifically to a *message dream*, as the
word *enypnion* does (Matthew 1:20; 2:12–13, 19, 22; 27:19; Acts
2:17; Jude 8). The expression "night vision" or "vision in the
night" is another phrase meaning *message* (Isaiah 29:7; Daniel
2:19; Acts 16:9, 18:9).

Scholars categorize biblical dreams in three primary divisions:
symbolic, literal, or prophetic. I've had dreams in all three
categories. Interestingly, sometimes the dream can be a
combination of two, but we have already established that dreams
provide insight and pertinent information or understanding of
something unknown or not commonly known. In other words, a
dream is a revelation of things that one would not know through
any natural means. It is always a word of knowledge, and it can be
prophetic. I've researched, talked to others, and had too many
dreams to believe otherwise.

Quite naturally, I often dream about my children, but I also dream
about the children of friends and children I do not know. Many
dreams have been about babies, parents, the elderly, the sick, the
deceased, and people around the globe. I have awakened from

dreams laughing out loud or weeping. I've dreamed about friends and enemies, jobs, businesses, houses and buildings, indecision and decision-making, churches and ministries, countries and constellations, and animals and insects, to name a few. The subjects are too many to list here.

I've heard songs during my dreams and recorded a few of them on two albums: "Praise Is Awaiting You" and "Glimpse."

It is not unusual for a literal dream to be revealed first and then develop a deeper spiritual meaning. God is concerned with every area and circumstance of our lives as His beloved children. He never does anything the same. Just as His mercies are new every morning, so are the ways He reveals Himself to us through dream types and interpretations.

Symbolic Dreams

Dreams often place us in unfamiliar surroundings full of symbols, imagery, and objects. They may include characters who are familiar to us or ones that we do not know. A hidden meaning or truth is revealed in interpreting the dream, imparting to the dreamer a broader message.

For example, let's look at King Nebuchadnezzar's experience recorded in Daniel 2. He had a dream that troubled him greatly. He saw a giant statue made of gold, silver, bronze, and iron mixed with clay. Then a stone struck the statue, breaking it into pieces. The wind carried the fragments away, leaving no traces behind.

The king did not recognize anyone in the dream, and we have no clear indication of the statue's location. This dream was both symbolic and prophetic. The king did not tell anyone about the dream but insisted that his astrologers and magicians tell him the dream and its interpretation. By means of divine revelation, Daniel explained to the king that the statue represented four successive kingdoms based upon power and wealth, beginning with Babylon. At the same time, the stone and mountain signified a kingdom established by God that would never be destroyed nor given to other people. Here is an example of a dream I have had in this category.

Dream

I am standing under two huge trucks parked very close together. Dust, debris, grit, and small squares of paper swirl around like a dust storm. It doesn't get in my eyes or mouth or go over my head.

Interpretation: Dixie

Whatever storm Satan stirs up, the Lord will supply you with more than enough protection to cover you and keep you from harm or damage. It will not affect your spiritual vision, speech, thinking, or wisdom. Stay in the position into which the Lord leads you, standing for Him and truth. He is your refuge amid the storm.

Literal Dreams

A literal dream is very specific and particular. For the most part, it includes no imagery or symbolic elements other than the event taking place. A literal dream comes true exactly as it happened and needs little or no interpretation.

Dream

A man I know named Eric, dressed in a dark suit, is standing near me. There is no conversation or movement. We are simply standing next to each other.

Fulfillment

Three days later, after our Sunday morning worship service, Eric, wearing a dark suit, stood near me as I prayed for his wife. In the dream, I did not see that we were in the church, nor did I see myself praying, but I saw Eric standing beside me as I had seen him in the dream. In other words, the setting for the dream may be slightly different from what occurs, but what transpires in reality will be in perfect alignment with the dream.

Dream

I am looking at a picture book that has big pages. The first time I look, the book doesn't lie flat. On the pages, I see two trucks with semi-trailers, one on either side of the page but side by side. They are both turned as if going north. I turn to the next page. The truck on the left is coming over onto the right side of the page, aimed at the end of the other truck.

Two days later, I turned on the TV and saw a news report that two semi-trucks had collided on the interstate highway. One had stopped for (at that time) an unknown reason; the other semi ran into the back of the stopped truck. The report later said there were injuries, but none were considered life-threatening.[2]

Prophetic Dreams

Prophetic dreams have been a topic of fascination and study for centuries, and they are often considered a form of extrasensory perception or precognition. These dreams are believed to provide insights into future events or offer guidance to individuals. However, it's essential to note that the scientific community generally approaches prophetic dreams with skepticism, as the phenomenon lacks empirical evidence and cannot be reliably tested or proven. However, in the faith community, we read otherwise in the biblical accounts, and those of us who record and date our dreams maintain records of God's faithfulness to show us something days, weeks, months, or years before it happens.

Prophetic dreams are often characterized by the following features:

- Vividness and Memorability: Prophetic dreams tend to be exceptionally vivid and memorable, making them stand out from regular dreams.
- Clarity: People who experience prophetic dreams often report that the dream's content is clear and coherent, making it easier to remember and interpret.

- Specificity: Prophetic dreams are believed to contain specific details about future events, such as locations, people, or objects.
- Emotional Intensity: These dreams can be emotionally charged, evoking strong feelings and reactions.
- Subsequent Realization: The dreamer may only recognize the prophetic nature of the dream after the predicted event has occurred.
- Variability: Prophetic dreams can cover a wide range of topics, from personal matters to global events.

Dream

A Sudanese man and I talk while I drive him to various places. I am trying to encourage this refugee. I take him to his apartment and give him a sweet potato pie that my son Keifer or I had made. I say, "You need to try this pie." He takes it, breaks part off, and takes a bite. I say, "Fine, you can have the rest later."

Interpretation: Dixie
You will have the opportunity to help a refugee or a group of them. You will give help and encouragement, prepare and offer spiritual teaching or advice for his or their

consumption and application. This dream emphasizes service and ministry to a foreign entity in the name of the Lord.

Fulfillment:

The outcome of this dream is so exciting. I had the dream on March 14, 2020, and Dixie's interpretation gave me the idea that I might work in a missions environment. God had a different plan in mind. By October 2022, I had all but forgotten this dream when I introduced myself to a young man visiting our church. He told me he was a student from South Sudan. I found myself blurting out, "I will be a mother to you while you are here."

True to my word, I picked him up from the home of the host family he was living with and drove him to see a few sights around our city. We stopped to get something to eat and then went to my home for tea. While we were conversing, he shared with me the harshness of growing up in a refugee camp. As a young man, he often prayed and wondered why he couldn't be like the other children and have someone tell him, "I am your mother; you are my son." That touched my heart. Not long after that, we were at dinner with some friends, and there was sweet potato pie for dessert. Perhaps you've guessed by now that all of the pie was not eaten, and my question to him was, "Would you like to take this pie home? You can eat it later."

Had I not been in the middle of research for this book and going through the long list of dreams I've recorded, I don't know that I would have recalled this dream. But I could not help but weep for joy for a God who would allow me the privilege of becoming a mother to a son far away and this being His divine plan, although it took two years for my dream to be fulfilled.

Dream

My older second cousin Paul T. is usually flamboyant in his yellow or bright pink suits. He and his wife dress in similar outfits. She is always by his side, but this time, she is not with him. I am in a building, where there is a conference going on, when Paul T. shows up dressed in all black. He speaks with some of my friends as if he knows them. As we go to another room for an event, another of my friends, Harrison, and Paul approach each other and start talking. I am surprised that Paul knows him and some of the others.

Interpretation: Dixie

The fact that his wife is usually with him, and she is not in this dream, and he is dressed in total black, which might indicate mourning, suggests his wife has passed away.

Fulfillment:

I had this dream May 25, 2022, and his wife passed away in the fall of 2022.

Symbols and Images

Details in dreams are important. Sometimes, we need to go back over the dream details to specify what we saw—people, animals, feelings, colors, words, objects, scene descriptions, etc.—that might be relevant. In following this process, you may discover a word or phrase that will be crucial to the interpretation. Paying attention to the details will help you learn to be diligent about the elements without disbelieving in God's purpose.

Vision

I am in worship, spending time in prayer. I see an enormous goblet suspended above the floor very high up—at least eight feet—in a church sanctuary. Water is pouring very deliberately into the goblet in slow motion, none splashing. It fills the goblet to the brim, but the water doesn't stop. It overflows, little streams of water flowing off the sides. Underneath that goblet are four or five other goblets, a little smaller, maybe six feet high. When they are filled to the brim, their overflow streams are smaller. At the last, the goblets are the same size. Some water streams forcibly, and some is slower, even trickling. Some goblets receive only a drop or two. These goblets, staggered, fill the sanctuary. No water spills on the floor.

Interpretation: Dixie and Mari

In the feeding of the five thousand, the overflow of bread and fish were collected in baskets so nothing would be wasted. The water is the Spirit of God pouring out His anointing on Mari, who is going to sing Saturday at a conference where an international speaker will teach. Those who attend with ready hearts will receive and nothing—not one drop—will be wasted. The size of the goblets represents the levels of spiritual maturity.

Fulfillment:

After the conference ended, one of the attendees approached me to share her joy at hearing me sing.

She stated, "As you sang it's as if you gave us a gift that we continued to unwrap during your song."

Conclusion

As you read this book, do you wonder how to increase your ability to dream or interpret? Are you asking yourself, "How do I start? Where do I begin?"

We cannot forcibly create a dream; it will have to happen naturally. However, you can create the spiritual atmosphere and environment necessary to hear from God. I encourage you to minimize online and other media distractions in the hours leading up to bedtime. Instead of staying up late watching movies or scrolling through social media, actively pursue and spend time in the presence of God. He has already promised that if we seek Him, we will find Him (Jeremiah 29:13). Throughout the day, read and meditate on His Word, and engage in conversations with Him. These actions reflect your genuine desire and willingness to communicate with the Lord. The rest is up to Him as He fans the flames of your gifts and guides you in your journey of faith.

The same principle applies to dream interpretation. Additionally, ask God for opportunities to practice this skill—whether it's interpreting your own dreams or those of others. Physical exercise is vital for the growth and development of our bodies; the same holds true for nurturing and expanding our spiritual gifts.

In the previous chapters, I have shared a few of my dreams with their interpretations. Now, let's take the first steps toward understanding dreams. To help you get started, you'll find two of my dreams for you to interpret. I've placed the interpretations at the back of the book after the section titled "Learning to Interpret."

My Prayer for You,

I pray that the Father would ignite a fiery passion within your heart for dreaming. I pray that you will be unwavering in your commitment to prayer, continually seeking more dreams and vivid recollections of them. I pray for your unwavering boldness and unshakeable confidence in God's boundless ability and His promise to exceed our greatest imaginings.

May you be abundantly blessed with someone gifted in interpreting dreams, and may this divine gift flourish and overflow in the service of His kingdom, shining brilliantly for God's glory.

I pray in Jesus's name, Amen

Learning to Interpret

Here are a few first steps to get you started in the process of interpreting dreams. See how you do. Test your skills with these steps and then check the interpretations.

List of Steps:

- Begin by praying for the Holy Spirit to reveal the meaning of the dream.

- Read the dream three or four times, allowing specific phrases or words to catch your attention—whether in consecutive readings or intermittently.

- Pay attention to any emotions or shifts in attitude that the dream portrays.

- Remember that the dream's narrative is an earthly story that carries a profound heavenly significance.

- Seek guidance from the Holy Spirit through scripture.

- Observer versus participant: If the dreamer is an observer, the interpretation will show you a revelation or teaching for someone else. Look at the position of the characters in the story. If you are in your house in your dream, it will likely be about you or your church and involve you. If it concerns someone else's house, it will affect their life. If you need a bathroom or are in a bathroom, it could mean there are areas in your life that need cleansing, or eliminating, or that you are cautious about living an unspotted life and need to take time to address potential problem areas before they manifest.

Try to interpret the following dreams. Interpretations are given at the end of the "Appendix of Dreams and Visions." You will also find pages for note-taking.

Bulldozer in the Lake

I am sitting on my deck and see a bulldozer going down the middle of the lake behind my house. It is parting the waters. I watch it go 25 feet to the right of my property, leaving dry land behind it. Eventually, it travels the entire length of my property.

Write Your Interpretation:

Rain-soaked Bible

Torrents of rain have fallen. When the rain stops, I look out the window and decide to take a walk. I am shocked and somewhat horrified to see my Bible has been left out in the rain. I rush over to pick it up. It is completely soaked through and through, swollen with water but firmly intact. Oddly, I see that it is full of water, but when I lift it off the ground, the water doesn't run off or out of the Bible, but somehow remains in it.

Write Your Interpretation:

Testimonials of Dreams and Visions

Testimonial

I was definitely blessed, touched, and encouraged by your dream of seeing my picture on a disc with the words "faithful and consistent" written on the back, and you feeling the word *beautiful* was a description of me. I remember feeling God's presence as I read your email, interpretation, and scripture suggestion of Song of Solomon. I read straight through the book, and I felt affirmation of Jesus's love for me and His kind, sweet, and encouraging words to me! I felt lifted up and encouraged and will do my best to stand firm on His truths and convicting words. What a gift your dream and interpretation have given me to show me how much God loves me and is encouraging me to stay faithful and consistent. Thank you, dear friend!

Note: Read Sallie's vision in the "Appendix of Dreams and Visions."

Blessings and love,

Sallie Winter

December 2019

Testimonial

You might have heard from my mom that I moved to New York! It all happened quite suddenly and hilariously, and I'm still not totally sure what I'm doing here, but I'm very thankful and overwhelmed with gratitude. I have read over what you saw for me a few times and felt confirmed that God wants me here. It's good for those days that I doubt myself. :) Thank you again for sharing your vision with me. It has continued to be a source of encouragement. I had no idea there would be a fulfillment so soon! I was thinking decades down the road but apparently God wanted me here NOW.

Note: Read Robin's vision in the "Appendix of Dreams and Visions."

Love,

Robin H.

October 2020

Testimonial

Mari dreamed in January, 2021, that we were seated at a small table side by side. We both had lemonade. We have since been teammates in a business venture and are finding working together very refreshing.

Amanda Chambers

Note: Find the details of Amanda's dream in chapter 4.

Testimonial

Your vision confirmed a decision that Lorin and I had already made and communicated to Holy Trinity Church about our departure from the church. At that time, God was calling us away to have space to continue pressing into Him about our next ministry assignment.

You also shared with us a vision you had while I preached at my last healing service at Holy Trinity. You saw a darker shade on top of me replaced with a bright picture of the armor of God. You interpreted it to mean that God was preparing us for a battle of His choosing. This vision resonated with us as God has used spiritual battle imagery to prepare and encourage us—especially in the current season we are in of waiting on Him. The day after you shared this vision with us, I was getting ready to drive Henry to school. Suddenly, I was overwhelmed with the love of God. The question that prompted it all was, "How loving is our God that He would share an encouraging message for me!" (through you).

In Christ,

Sam Sholander

March 2020

Testimonial

You shared a dream that I was ministering alongside you, and someone was heavily resting in the Holy Spirit, but was trying to get back up. You told the person, "Just stay down there and keep receiving from the Lord!" Then you turned around, and I was trapped back in a corner—there was a closet, a rocking chair, and a desk. I was not happy. You pulled out the rocking chair in such a way that it blocked me from coming back out into the ministry area, but still giving me freedom, and making the chair available for me to sit in. The closet was for hiding—this is a prayer closet time. The rocking chair is for rest. The desk is for study or learning from the Lord. It has been an accurate indicator for the season I just came through. The Lord firmly pulled me out of ministry and set me in a "prayer closet" season with rest and learning. You were spot on.

Cynthia Harris
November 2019

Testimonial

I have been writing short stories and articles for at least two decades but continued to have doubts about my writing abilities. Mari's dream in 2020 about me winning a prize was not only encouraging but let me know God was highlighting my desire to have my work receive more exposure. Since the dream, I've written an essay that is included in an anthology and have won a scholarship to a prestigious Christian writer's conference. I am so thankful God continues to speak to us through dreams and to Mari for allowing the Dream Giver to use her gift.

Kim H. M.

Testimonial

Mari sent me a dream she had. I believe it pointed to a significant hurt my husband (a pastor) and I were about to experience in ministry. One month later, our world unraveled. In that season, when I felt betrayed and forgotten, the dream reminded me that God sees me and knows everything about my situation. Recently, Mari had another dream that included diapers. Our three children are far past that stage, but I believe the dream showed the redemption of God happening in our lives. A new ministry and new hope are being birthed in our lives.

Mari has also been able to interpret many dreams I have had over the past twenty-five years. Her gift of having and interpreting dreams has helped me to hear and understand what God was saying to me in critical junctures of my life.

Jamie Stewart

FAQs

Q: I know I have dreams, but sometimes I forget what they are about. What if I miss something God is trying to show me?

A: There have been numerous instances when I didn't recall a dream in its entirety, yet I sensed its significance. And there were times when I completely forgot a dream upon waking. My experience has shown me that the Holy Spirit will bring the dream back to my remembrance when it's most needed. I've been in situations, and suddenly, the Holy Spirit will make me aware that I've dreamt about what is happening around me.

Q: Why are all my dreams nonsensical?

A: Keep in mind that messages are occasionally concealed. The seemingly nonsensical aspects might actually be the crucial pieces linking the dots of the puzzle. Never cast aside a dream because it does not make sense to you. This is where prayer and faith work together.

Q: Why do some people think all dreams are divinely inspired?

A: I firmly believe the majority of our dreams come from divine inspiration. A small fraction might be influenced by other factors. Strengthening my faith through seeking dreams has amplified the spiritual significance of my dreams, setting them apart from mere observations.

Q: Are dreams from God always good?

A: Indeed, dreams from God are not negative, regardless of the scenario. While dreams aren't exactly scriptures like the written Word (*logos*), they are a form of God's communication (*rhema*). They are bestowed upon the dreamer and conveyed to interpreters.

The Holy Spirit often brings certain applicable Bible verses to mind that are meant to accompany and support the interpretation. Believers who immediately jump to a doubt-centric outlook will bring up the possibility of a devil-implanted dream. They need to understand Psalm 3:3, "The LORD is my shield" and 1 Corinthians 2:16, "We have the mind of Christ" (in our spirit). The Lord is the shield of my mind, and as I sleep, He protects it.

Even scary dreams can be warnings, alerts from the Lord, and the exposing of satanic plans. Initially, when I told Dixie a dream, I sometimes introduced it as a "bad one." But the interpretation always brought a positive message. The dream may instruct, reveal, encourage, warn, inform, etc., but it also brings you privileged communication from your King. That in itself makes the message divine and beneficial.

Q: How can I be sure I hear an interpretation correctly?

A: Engaging in Spirit-led prayer can refine your ability to perceive. On a certain day, while walking laps at a nearby high school track, Dixie prayed in her prayer language (Ephesians 6:18, Jude 1:20). Later that day, I shared a dream with her. She noticed that praying in the Spirit had heightened her receptivity and sensitivity to His voice (1 Corinthians 14:4), enabling her to receive the interpretation even before I completed describing the dream.

Q: If a dream is a warning, what should I do?

A: Prayer has the potential to influence outcomes. When other avenues seem limited, prayer remains a powerful choice. If a dream's scenario doesn't materialize, it could result from the dreamer and interpreter praying for a change in the person's mindset, repentance, or an extension of mercy and time. United prayer between the dreamer and interpreter stands as a strong stance in spiritual warfare. (See The Train Dream in Chapter 6.)

Appendix of Dreams and Visions

Here is an alphabetical listing of a few of the dreams I've had through the years.

Allegorical Dreams

My Son Raking

I see different sections—whether it is two plots of vacant land or a building surrounded by land is unclear. The ground is littered with fallen leaves, and there are three distinct areas that need raking or clearing. I know about these three spots, and they are all visible at once. My son Keifer stands nearby, rake in hand. I approach him and ask, "Where did you rake? Where did you work?" He points toward one of the sections, and I nod in approval. "That's good. That was the right place."

Interpretation: Dixie
Keifer will have three choices for work, he will choose the right one, and you will confirm that to him.

Fulfillment
I had this dream in January 2019, and in March 2019 Keifer was offered his dream job, but it was only for a year. He wasn't sure if he should look for something with more job security, but we were

both convinced he'd enjoy the job, and it would be a worthwhile experience.

My son Keifer writes: "My mom's dreams have terrified, blessed, inspired, and guided me. They were strange but specific, but perhaps most inconceivable, they were true. God speaks to my mom. I know that now."

Animals

Dog in the Sky

I look up in the sky and see an enormous frame with the profile of a standing dog. I realize why the dog is so shiny; it is made entirely of silver ball chains. A person with a big plastic cup goes to the frame in the sky and puts the cup at the corner of the frame. The ball chains start unraveling slowly. A stream of chains flows, but the dog never loses its form until it disappears into the cup.

Interpretation: Scott (Dixie's brother)
The dog represents a deception. Something will be released on the earth but hindered by what the chain represents, so it will be restrained and never lose the restraint until the end. It cannot and does not have influence over the saint of faith who walks in Christ's authority. The Lord is giving you this revelation to pray

for understanding. Agree with the Lord over what it involves and for faith to overcome.

Biting Cats

I'm with someone, and we go to a basement apartment. I'm at the door talking with the woman who lives there; she is someone I know. I see a huge gray cat at her feet, rubbing against her leg and purring, but the cat growls at me. I tell the woman about it, and she says the cat doesn't always act that way. I am startled. The cat edges toward the door and bares its teeth at me, so I back away from the doorway, but the woman keeps talking. Then, swiftly and unexpectedly, the cat leaps at me. I turn and run into the next apartment's open door, but the cat gets in that door. I see long, felt cloth toys with animal heads and glued-on eyes that are eight to ten inches long scattered on the floor. I jump on a chair to avoid the cat, and the toys begin to move toward me with razor-sharp teeth. My heart races as I feel the unnatural bite of the cloth animals closing on my hand. I scream for the owner to come to get the attacking cat. The woman says, "OK," but takes her time getting there. The cloth animals bite me, and I feel them clamping down on my hand. I feel pressure but no pain. I try to pry the animals' mouths open to free my hand.

Interpretation: Dixie

The huge growling cat means the attack, opposition, antagonism, or pressure will be pronounced and joined by others. The cat represents someone closely associated with the woman. However, they will have no lasting effects. "The cat doesn't always act that way" means its real feelings or heart is concealed from others. In the atmosphere of your anointing, the ugliness of an ungodly person will be revealed. Remember, self-righteous people won't admit their sins and will not repent.

Fulfillment

Over time, this situation and person were shown to me.

Blessings

Overflowing Grocery Bag

Opening my front door, I am met with an unexpected sight—a bag of groceries standing upright on the porch as if it has been placed there with deliberate care. Interestingly, what strikes me is the way the groceries are stacked inside the bag. It is as if they are defying gravity—some items protruding gracefully beyond the rim by a mere couple of inches.

Interpretation: Dixie

Provisions, pressed down and almost running over the bag's edges, whether natural or spiritual, will be a gift from the Lord. It will represent the blessings of the Lord being passed on to you. Don't see yourself as doing without (soulishness); watch for the Lord's provisions (spirit). They will always show up, even unexpectedly.

Cakes

I find myself at a lively function, surrounded by an assortment of delectable cakes. There are two distinct varieties that tantalize the senses:

Yellow Cake with Swirls of Buttercream Icing and Pecans: These cakes are adorned with intricate swirls of buttercream icing, topped with crunchy pecans. Each slice is meticulously cut to display the mesmerizing swirl patterns.

Chocolate Cake with Chocolate Ganache and Fresh Berries: Another delicious option is the chocolate cake, generously coated with rich chocolate ganache and adorned with whole strawberries or raspberries. The berries are not just a garnish; they mingle with the luscious ganache, creating a burst of fruity flavor.

Some cakes are presented as layered masterpieces, while others take the form of simple sheet cakes. The portions vary in size, offering something for everyone. Guests eagerly gather around the dessert table, each person selecting a slice that suits their preference.

I can't decide and sample both varieties. The flavors dance on my taste buds, and I savor every bite.

After indulging in these sweet delights, I venture into the next room, which turns out to be a gymnasium. In one corner, I observe a group of guys shooting hoops. The connection between the two rooms is filled with tables, and to my amazement, the tables have pockets like pool tables and display even more cakes.

These cakes in the pockets are unique—cylindrical in shape. Instead of a net, the cake extends downward. I can't resist the urge to sample this intriguing creation. I slice off a portion from the bottom of one of the pocket cakes to taste.

Filled with contentment, I return to the first room to indulge in yet more of the delightful cakes, enjoying each moment of this sweet adventure.

Interpretation: Dixie

The yellow cake represents the glory available to all Christians, and the chocolate one represents the bounty of the fruit produced by the Holy Spirit working in and through you. The glory and the bounty are both available for consumption and appropriation (2 Corinthians 3:18). Some opportunities will be small, some large. The gym and the pool tables are places or opportunities and activities to refine your skills in perhaps unlikely ways—not necessarily church-oriented. Again, when you partake of what God has provided for you, your appetite for more increases. You were insatiable in the dream. You wanted more and more—such a beautiful quality of your faith, not only to believe but also to expect wonderful results from your consumption of these cakes.

Children

Hidden Baby Carrier

I'm in my neighbor Teresa's van. Teresa is in the back seat with one of her sons; the other son is the driver. The seats are covered with a dingy silver cloth; most of the shine has worn off. When the engine starts, I look for my seat belt but can't find it. I lift the seat cover, which goes to the floor to find my seat belt. Instead, I find a tiny baby girl in a car carrier. Dressed in pink, she has a cute little round face. This unexpected discovery sends a rush of surprise through me. My heart races.

Fulfilment

The following day, I saw Teresa. (I hadn't seen her in at least two years.) Remembering the dream, I asked if she had a granddaughter. She beamed and said, "Yes, she's four weeks old. Born in 2023, she's the first granddaughter in the family in two generations ." This dream was a sweet word of knowledge, confirmed by my conversation with Teresa.

Direction

Edward and Friends Clear the Way

I am in my car coming home. I drive onto the porch. Something blocks my intention of going over the porch to the driveway side. My husband Edward and some men come out and tell me I can't go any farther. I peer out of my car window, assessing the predicament and the prospect of reversing my car to get out of this tight spot. I say, "I think it will damage my car."

I remember we have a two-door garage in the back. I ask Edward and the men if they will clear the space and open the garage. They move miscellaneous furniture, barrels, boxes, etc. As the clutter disappears, the garage's two large doors creak open, enabling me to drive through the garage, out the other side, and back around to the front driveway.

Interpretation: Dixie

The Lord gives you another path, an unusual one, to get to your desired destination. Some things will need to be cleared first. He will provide just what you need, including the people to help you achieve the goal.

Difference between Spirit and Soul

I am in a classroom filled with four or five women seated together. One of them begins expressing her discouragement, how down her spirit feels. I gently offer a correction, saying, "That isn't truly your spirit. Your spirit is always aligned with the Holy Spirit, and He's never down." I explain the distinction between the soul (comprising intellect, will, and emotions) and the spirit. Dixie, seated on the adjacent side, chimes in, "That's absolutely right." This dream played out in Mari's meeting before she told Dixie the dream. We had discussed spirit-soul-body principles several times.

Encouragement

I am sitting at a round café table with another woman. We are talking, and I am thrilled and having a great time and conversation.

Fulfillment:
Amazingly, this dream was fulfilled on the same evening of August 20 in a conversation on the phone with Dixie as we talked about many different spiritual topics, which encouraged and uplifted both of us.

Enemies

I have been in hiding and, for some reason, I am able to come out and meet with my friends. We are all happy to see each other. I am moving cautiously, afraid of being detected. The people who have held me captive, or are looking for me, come into the room. Most of those in the room are lying down, and a few are watching TV or just sitting around.

I get down on the floor too. I put a cover over my face. The people are looking at everyone else's faces. A woman comes over, pulls my blanket off ever so slightly, looks at me, and continues on. I overhear my enemies say, "She's not here. Let's go."

After a short time, I get up. I decide to pack my things and leave. As I walk through the room, another young woman comes in and is happy to see me. She says, "I'm so glad Mari's back," which alerts those who have been looking for me. When they hear her, they rush back into the room.

I run up the steps, and find two cabinets. One has a secret compartment. I take four to five items out to make room. I realize I am emptying the wrong cabinet. I put a few things back but then start taking things out of the second secret compartment, preparing to hide again.

Interpretation: Dixie

Jesus is your hiding place (Psalm 32:7). Though you forget that in the dream for a moment, you remember the scripture that says, "The LORD is a strong tower. The righteous run to it and are safe" (Proverbs 18:10 NKJV). You are to hide in Jesus and let Him be your shield. Let Him do the fighting, and you do the trusting.

Fear

I step outside into the tranquility of my yard and spot an iridescent hummingbird darting toward a cluster of blossoms.

Mesmerized, I turn my gaze toward it, only to have it abruptly veer toward me and attack me, colliding with my head and becoming entangled in my hair. Panic surges through me, and I scream. The person by my side rushes to my aid, attempting to free the frantic bird from my hair.

I reach out with trembling fingers, gingerly trying to grasp the delicate creature, holding it gently between my index and middle fingers while using my thumb to support its fragile body. The once-graceful wings of the hummingbird fall down to the ground like toothpicks, little by little, gradually disintegrating. The agonizing sound of its wings tearing of being ensnared in my hair echoes in my ears.

Interpretation: Dixie
Even a small attack of evil intent is startling. However, you and a helper quickly take control, capture it, and cast it out as it falls apart and brings no harm to you.

Glory

I'm at a monastery. We're on break at a conference. We venture outdoors. The monastery is nestled in a valley, and as we leave the confines of the building, a steep hill welcomes us.

It is foggy as we reach the top, but the lake's palette of dark purples, blues, and grays can still be discerned. A young woman with me keeps walking when I pause to bask in the foggy beauty a while longer. A gentle breeze begins to blow, and as if in response, the fog gradually lifts, revealing the lake in all its splendor. I stop to look at the beauty of the lake.

The fog lifts little by little. It forms a cloud, which comes toward me. I call my friend to come witness this fascinating sight. I eagerly position myself directly in the cloud's path. It hits me with a thud rather than passing me like a mist. The small cloud comes near again. I place myself in the direct path of the cloud so it will hit me again with the same exciting impact.

My friend is at the top of a brick staircase overlooking the area and calls me to come to where she is. I go up to the red brick stairs, enclosed on both sides with brick walls. Instead of the foggy cloud, I encounter a delightful surprise. Every step is adorned with cloud-like snow resembling thick, soft lace. It is beautiful and soft to the touch.

I put my hand on it. I want to show this to Dixie, so I ask my friend to take a picture. Instead, she puts her cell phone within my reach. I delicately pull some of the pristine white snow-lace from the steps, savoring its beauty.

It is so divine. I can't describe it. It must be manna, I think. I taste it, and it is sweet, like whipped honey. I climb a few more steps, not to the top, but high enough to see all around. The view and the experience are nothing short of glorious.

Interpretation: Dixie

You will take a break and be open to ascending to a higher level, where you will enjoy your surroundings and see more of the artistry of God the Creator. You will experience the cloud of His Presence and be enveloped by it. You will be fed a little of the heavenly manna, which is thought to be able to sustain a person far longer than ordinary food. "To the one who is victorious, I will give some of the hidden manna" (Revelation 2:17 NIV).

When you must return to the lower level, there will be things in place to make your transition easier, a way to make the food of the Word more digestible.

Houses

Mari's House Renovation, December 2019

There is a major renovation project underway at my house. I am in the living room, and water drips from the ceiling. Workers are trying to decide the best attack on it.

I go into a bedroom. Young people are taking framed pictures from the collage off the wall. I ask, "Where are the pictures you took down?" No one knows. I say, "I didn't ask for this to be done." Their supervisor comes in, and I tell her I want the pictures tracked down as soon as possible.

The supervisor tells me who is in charge of the young people, but she doesn't know where
he is. She leaves the room, and I walk out behind her. There are lots of people working; the hallway is crowded. I find the person in charge, and he doesn't know about the pictures. I am frustrated. They are working in the kitchen, and I spot a place that has been cemented in cinder blocks, where a doorway had been. A window has been blocked too. The rest of the kitchen looks great, with new windows and doors.

Looking at the work and walking through the house, I go to the huge garage, where someone is cutting wood on a sawhorse. From the garage, there are stairs up to the house. I walk up the steps and look into the master bedroom. It is lovely.

Interpretation: Dixie
This dream speaks of unexpected changes, which will remove some of the old ways of doing things (blocked door), will alter old

ways of looking at things (blocked window), and bring freedom from things of your past (pictures) that need to be let go. It will be a strange time, even disconcerting, in that you don't really want to let some of these things go, but the new sights and ways of going in and out will be very pleasing and more than satisfactory in the end. You will have plenty of help in doing this at the appropriate times. "Trust in the LORD with all your heart and do not lean on your own understanding" (Proverbs 3:5 ESV).

Fulfillment
This dream has both spiritual and literal aspects to it. By God's grace, surprise, and a miracle, my house was completely renovated in October 2020!

Ideas and Designs

Journal Designs
One evening while praying, I asked the Lord to give me an idea for income. That night I had this dream:

I see a thick journal, the size of a thin Bible, with gold-leaf edges on the pages. The Lord shows me a design on the cover of a journal, using wire and beads, etc. One design is visible, and then another design replaces it. This happens three or four times with different designs.

The next day I found the exact type of journals I'd seen in the dream, created stunning covers for them, then placed them in my online store.

Jewelry Disks

As I'm on my way to meet my friend Kim, I unexpectedly encounter an acquaintance who excitedly shares her latest creative venture: crafting jewelry disks from wood. I admire her sister's outfit and jewelry, and can't help but comment on its beauty. However, her sister quickly interjects, cautioning me not to touch the jewelry, only to admire it from a distance. The woman then proudly displays two of her wooden disks suspended from a necklace, each adorned with delicate flowers and lace-like patterns drilled into the wood. Struggling to see the intricate details, I tell her, "I can't see them very well," prompting her to let me touch them. In response, I mention that I create a similar design using polymer clay.

Interpretation: Mari
This showed me another design for jewelry making.

Kitchens

I'm cooking with a group of people, and they ask me if they can taste my food. I feel like we are in a contest. They keep peering into my pot but don't let me see or taste their food.

Interpretation: Dixie
There is a judgmental spirit of competition that comes with these deceitful people. They want to see and get some of your knowledge and teaching but won't share theirs because they know theirs is not entirely up to par with yours. They may even try to pass on your teachings as if they were their own.

Learning

Someone has written a report, just as I have done. However, their text is typed in a smaller font with strategic bolding, while mine is in a larger font without any boldface. Intrigued, I ask, "How did you achieve that effect?" The person explains that they pressed down with their entire palm on the printed paper as it came out of the printer. This action reduces the font size and adds emphasis to specific words. Eager to try it myself, I follow their advice, and to my amazement, it works.

Interpretation:Dixie

The Lord, possibly through a person, shows you how to use your power to change something for the better. What it involves is simple, but has an application you had never tried or even imagined.

Ministry

I'm a passenger in a Jeep that I'm sharing with someone. We are happy. I comment that having a Jeep to go over any terrain is nice. My friend, the driver, agrees. The driver may be Dixie. We immediately leave the smooth road and turn onto rough, rugged patches of land and drive up a grassy hill. Trees are all around, and there is no paved road through it, so we are making a road with the Jeep. We go up and down other hills many times, and it is fun.

Then we come to a very steep place. We go straight down, hit the Jeep's front bumper, and then the vehicle straightens and lands on all four tires. I look back and see a long, thick chain behind us. A trailer is hitched to the Jeep. I say, "We can't bring the trailer; it's at the top of the steep incline, while the Jeep is at the bottom."

We unhitch the chain and pull the trailer along a side passage. There are tree limbs and fallen logs on that side, and we pull the wagon over them until we arrive at the bottom. There are people in the wagon, two rows of four people all upright, but by the time the wagon hits the ground, the people are spread out but not hurt. We plan to hitch the wagon to the Jeep and keep traveling.

Interpretation: Dixie
God supplies us with a ministry capable of working in any circumstance, smooth or rough, paved or not. We let nothing stop us because we are confident in the ministry, the call He has given us and His purpose.

Music

I am walking down a rural road and hear the most beautiful music and singing I have ever listened to. I see a small church on a hill, and I am so drawn to the music, I follow the sound. Just as I approach the door to the church, the dream ends.

No interpretation needed.

Fulfillment
I had heard the song that was being sung in the dream enough times that I was singing it when I woke up. "Sing out the honor of His name; make His praise glorious. Say to God, 'How awesome

are Your works! Through the greatness of Your power Your enemies shall submit themselves to You. All the earth shall worship You and sing praises to You. They shall sing praises to Your name'" (Psalm 66:2–4 NKJV).

I've written over two hundred songs and recorded two CD albums from a myriad of song dreams like this one.

Nature

A woman is admiring my flowers. As I stand in my fragrant garden, I advise her to purchase them during a particular season, ensuring that they would bloom beautifully in the following one. I promise her a bouquet if she returns in the spring, but she hesitates, uncertain of her plans. In that moment, I pluck a magnificent blossom, delicately remove a stamen, and hand it to her.

Interpretation: Dixie
Someone has noticed and will admire your work in a particular area, and they can tell you excel. This person would like to know more about your work, desiring to have that same kind of understanding and expertise. You couldn't help her much because of limited time, but you give her the essence, the beginning

principles of your knowledge, and the key to continuing to grow in this area of endeavor.

Olives and Oil

I am given five or six olives in my hand. I dislike eating olives.

Interpretation: Scott
Olives are the beginning element of the anointing oil which, among other things, can be used for healing and or deliverance. Transforming olives into anointing oil takes time and requires a process to achieve the outcome, so don't turn the opportunity down even if it seems distasteful. Look past the olives to the outcome.

Prayer

I wake up in my bed and notice the light in the bathroom is flickering. I get up and go into the hallway to find the electrical panel. I push a button for the bath and the hall light to come back on—no flickering now. I see dim, soft lights in the dining and living rooms downstairs. I press another button—music begins to play. At first, the singing sounds like chipmunk voices; however, the voices gradually harmonize, becoming more precise, and the melody grows louder, resonating throughout the house. Attempting to manage the unexpected volume, I try to turn it down, but my efforts prove futile. The voices persist, repeating the chorus of the song in an insistent loop: "I found the answer; I learned to pray." The melody seems to seep into the walls, merging with the essence of the house, as if the walls themselves are alive with the sound.

Interpretation: Dixie

Spiritually, Mari is at rest in the Lord (in bed). She trusts Him for the night. When she is alerted to the fact that a person in her life is not burning brightly for the Lord but is in danger of going out, Mari finds the source of power—the Lord. Prayer is the key to helping that person or persons, and the song is an effective reminder .

Quarry Escape

As I stroll along the familiar road, I have a clear destination in mind. I know where I am going. However, my journey takes an unexpected turn when the street abruptly ends, depositing me at the entrance of a colossal rock quarry. Towering gray cliffs, tinged with traces of rust, surround me. The noise of heavy machinery echoes through the air. I keep walking, thinking I can get to the other side, but I find no way out. I have to turn and go back. Just before I turn around, I see a ledge path used for more drilling. I could climb on it, get out, and walk from one side to the other. A man's voice booms through a loudspeaker, commanding, "There goes some more trying to get across. Stop them."

I look down, and people are running out from where I entered. They are leaving, all heading in the same direction. I realize I must go. I keep going, passing through several rooms. I am relieved when I exit that place.

Interpretation: Dixie
The male leader, the voice of direction in the quarry, could make trouble but won't interfere as you leave because he doesn't recognize who you really are. He is too busy and, therefore, missed the visitation from the Lord's representative.

Rest

Blue Robe
It is intended to be a short practice for worship. I am going to play the drums and keyboard for one song. I am not going to sing.

A new woman plays the violin. It is horrible and off-tune, but the leaders let her finish the practice. I do not see the rest of the team, just the two male leaders. The church is filled with people for a service. I realize I am wearing my aqua blue bathrobe. I may have noticed my clothing during practice, but I didn't mind and wasn't embarrassed because I plan to go straight home and only our small group is present. But everyone else is dressed up. Strangely, no one mentions my clothing or looks at me oddly. I just couldn't believe how I had shown up.

Interpretation: Dixie

Your robe means rest. You are relaxed—no worries. That contentment and trust results in peace (Isaiah 26:3; Romans 15:13; Philippians 4:6–7). Blue represents the Holy Spirit and heaven, those who are working under His direction (Malachi 1:8). The violinist represents those who want to perform and be up front but who have nothing of value to give, and they do not honor the Lord in any way.

Singing

I am standing in front of a large group of people singing for an important person, perhaps a dignitary of some sort. After I finish singing, the ensuing worship makes me cry.

Fulfillment

That is one dream a painfully shy little girl with low self-esteem could not believe would ever happen. Decades later, I was asked to sing before a prominent ministry leader spoke. The place was packed.

Stories

Liriel

I dream about the beautiful story I am supposed to write about a mother and daughter. The words I hear in the dream are, "My name means perfect." My mother never explained it this way, but I believe it means perfect family, perfect life, because that's what I have. (Her journal entry).

Needs no interpretation.

Travel

Island Hopping

I'm traveling from place to place, perhaps an island. When I wake up, I am praying in Spanish.

Interpretation: Dixie

Pack your bags. Looks like you'll be traveling in the future. Better brush up on your Spanish!

Unity

Bags of Apples vision

I'm looking into the front seat of a car, and I see three five-pound bags of apples. Two are upright, and one has fallen over.

Interpretation: Dixie

This vision is about three leaders involved in ministry. All are in the front seat of the car. They are a team. All are fruitful in work. However, two are spiritually upright and one has fallen over because an unbalanced part caused them to fall. There is no indication of rottenness (sin), just imbalance in their life. Something has shifted and needs to be corrected.

Victory

I'm behind the wheel of a massive bus, either a city transit vehicle or a Greyhound coach. I confess to my daughter, Rooney, "I'm not particularly fond of driving buses. I'll be glad when we get where we're supposed to be." The bus struggles to pass a pedestrian on the driver's side, but I navigate cautiously. Suddenly, the road transforms into a staircase. The bus accelerates, and we are screaming as it descends twelve flights of treacherously icy steps, teetering on the brink above a body of water. With a safe stop achieved, happiness and relief wash over us. My daughter commends my driving skills. I tell her it wasn't my skill; it was the Holy Spirit. God was good to save us. Glancing in the rearview mirror, I spot an Amtrak train coming at us. Swiftly, I instruct my daughter to unbuckle her seat belt. Then I drive the bus off the cliff and into the water below. To our astonishment, the bus does not sink but remains afloat.

Interpretation: Dixie

"I'll be glad when we get where we're supposed to be" should be the mindset of every Christian. Period. Life is full of unexpected situations where we must move with caution and make choices of faith. The Lord will guide you through the restrictions and the danger. He will keep your ministry afloat when circumstances or people threaten it.

Warnings

Traffic signs

I see small flashes of different signals and also signs such as Yield, School Zone, and Stop. Then there are sheets of paper with words of warnings. Someone is also talking to me, giving me cautionary words.

Interpretation: Dixie

Traffic signs represent the Law, the Word of God, which will warn you how to proceed slowly so that you will not be involved in any accidents if you obey them, and no one else will be negatively impacted. Spoken or written warnings come from those who care about you, including the Holy Spirit. They will help you discern all you need to keep you from Satan's potholes and pitfalls and from hurting anyone in your path—"praying always with all prayer and supplication in the Spirit" (Ephesians 6:18 NKJV).

Washcloths

I was offered stacks of washcloths, striped or plain, large or small, about four in each set. I wasn't excited; I didn't care one way or the other.

Interpretation: Dixie

Notice in the dream you weren't excited. You know what's coming, and that the size, color, or fanciness of the means for cleansing will not matter. Those things do not contribute to the assignment. You get the offer of the washcloths, you are being given the authority to use them on those who need cleansing, or to distribute the knowledge of it, which will lead them to the place of a pure heart, clean spiritual hands and feet. Consider this an honor the Lord gives you. He trusts you and will lead you in it (John 13:10; Psalm 24:4).

Xenia (hospitality)

After a meeting concludes, a woman I recently met approaches me, inviting me to join her for lunch. Curious to know more about her and engage in conversation and fellowship, I accept the offer. We find a table and settle in for a meal.

As we converse, another lady makes her way over to us. She says, "Oh, you're having lunch. Do you mind if I join you?" She says she had intended to ask me to lunch earlier to get to know me better. Welcoming the company, she takes a seat at our table, adding to the growing camaraderie.

In a matter of minutes, two more women approach, seeking to be a part of the conversation. The group now numbers five, a lively mix of individuals engaging in shared moments over a meal.

Amidst the discussions and laughter, I glance around, noting a curious coincidence—each of us wears a blue dress, the color ranging from medium to royal blue. It is a delightful observation, adding an unexpected touch of unity to the afternoon encounter.

Interpretation: Dixie
What you are, spiritually and otherwise, will attract certain discerning women to you. They will be drawn to your light. You recognize the importance of the blue dresses as these women are, like you, learning to follow the guidance and leadership of the Holy Spirit. They will acknowledge you have the relationship and fellowship they are seeking. The variations of blue indicate the women will be at different stages or levels of the education the Holy Spirit is teaching.

Youth

Japanese School Girls Chorus
I am transported to a bustling marketplace in Japan, a vibrant scene filled with bolts of cloth reminiscent of batik rather than the usual

silk or satin. I am conversing fluently with the Japanese people. A lot of buying and selling is going on.

Then I see a procession of young Japanese girls clad in their distinctive black jumpers, white blouses, and black cardigans resembling school uniforms. They walk in unison, a single file of harmony, as they hum the familiar tune of "Jesus Loves Me." Someone is shushing them, but that only fortifies their resolve as they continue, their unified hums merging into a singular voice, echoing like a beautifully unique instrument.

Interpretation: Dixie
This is another picture of part of the world's younger generation who will turn to the Lord. You will become aware of this segment, perhaps within a specific ethnic group, who will be steadfast in their commitment to Him and will not listen to those who tell them to cease. They will be singularly united in their testimony for the Lord Jesus. While the world focuses on gain, this group will focus on the love of the Lord, and it will sustain them.

Zee's Bad Foot

I am talking to someone who reminds me of Zee, my car mechanic. We are walking together in a hallway of a building. He is walking rather oddly. I ask him if there is something wrong. He says, "Yes, I'm in a lot of pain." He is limping. I ask, "Why don't you take your shoe off?" He agrees and leans against a wall to do so. He says repeatedly, "Don't laugh, Mari, don't laugh." I can tell he doesn't want to be embarrassed.

He takes his shoe and sock off. His big toe is severely deformed—very large, curling downward—and another smaller toe underneath it is also curling downward. There is nothing to laugh about; I feel compassion for his plight. After I see his toes, he puts his arm around my shoulder, and I put mine around him to help him continue to walk.

Interpretation: Dixie and Mari

The Zee person is someone who ordinarily would not be looking for help or sympathy. He is a self-sufficient person and one who generally gives service to others. His painful problem has been hidden but is now growing more pronounced and affecting his spiritual walk more clearly. You will become aware of this painful condition and want to help him. You will counsel and support him as he deals with this situation, which has affected his balance and changed his walk for the Lord.

Visions

"For still the vision awaits its appointed time; it hastens to the end —it will not lie. If it seems slow, wait for it; it will surely come; it will not delay" (Habakkuk 2:3 ESV). Habakkuk's prayer of faith and the vision given by God in the midst of widespread destruction remain a powerful testament to us concerning our need for endurance and hope because of God's unwavering faithfulness. Habakkuk's willingness to write down what he saw certainly encourages and inspires us to do the same.

God speaking though His prophet Hosea said, "I have also spoken by the prophets, and I have multiplied visions, and used similitudes, by the ministry of the prophets" (Hosea 12:10 KJV).

Floating Heart

I see my heart and it is tethered, anchored to the ground with ropes and pegs, as a hot air balloon would be. I start praying, worshiping, and as I do, the ropes unfurl from the pegs one at a time. Eventually all the ropes are loose but still attached to my heart, which begins to float upward into the unlimited and beautiful sky.

Interpretation: Dixie and Mari

The things that have tied your heart to the earth will be gradually loosened until your heart is unfettered completely. Nothing will weigh you down. A hot air balloon is supposed to fly, and its beauty is in doing what it is designed to do. Nothing is going to keep you from that. You will fly with the Lord. As the scripture states, You will "mount up with wings as eagles" (Isaiah 40:31 KJV).

Communing with the Trinity

I am seated at a long banquet table with many, many others and the Trinity. Suddenly I rise high above the table. When I look down, the table is in the shape of a heart.

Ornate Bible

I see a book on a table. I say, "Oh, it's a Bible." It is significantly large—its cover ornate, with raised scrolls and swirls. It looks like patinaed copper with gold-leaf edged pages. When I pick it up, I know it is a Bible.

Interpretation: Dixie

Outwardly, you find something you recognize is from God and has been cherished as valuable. To you, His Word is more beautiful than ever before. It will seem like its glory and meaning are more enhanced than you have realized.

Ocean

I stand on a cliff looking down at the bluest still water I've ever seen. I feel the nudge to jump, but I am afraid, so I continue to stand at the edge. The nudge comes again, and the word *jump* is louder, so I close my eyes and jump off the cliff. I look to see how far down I'm falling, and instead of the vast ocean, I see two enormous cupped hands holding the water.

Sallie Winter

There are a lot of discs being strung on wires about two feet long, hanging from the ceiling. Pictures are on the front of the discs, and words are written on the backs. The only phrase I remember is "faithful and consistent." When I read the discs and look at the pictures, I add, "and beautiful!" The picture is of Sallie Winter.

Robin H.

A young woman stands in front of our congregation to say goodbye as she transitions from Children's Ministry Director. I have a vision of her holding an open book in her hand. She is superimposed upon a backdrop of massive skyscrapers. The Holy Spirit gives me the impression of three cities—Boston, Jerusalem, and New York City. When I share the vision with her, she exclaims, "I've always wanted to live in all three."

Dream Interpretations

How did you do interpreting the dreams given in "Learning to Interpret"?

Bulldozer in Lake Interpretation: Watching the Lord make the way and clear a path. I didn't have to do anything in my own strength.

Rain-Soaked Bible Interpretation: Rain represents blessings from heaven more than can be counted, innumerable. I walk into the rain by choice.

Endnotes

[1] "Is Cessationism Biblical? What Is a Cessationist?" Got Questions, accessed November 18, 2023, https://www.gotquestions.org/cessationism.html.

[2] *HOPE MILLS, N.C. (WNCN, WRAL) — Three people were injured when a tractor-trailer smashed into another along Interstate 95 south of Fayetteville on the morning of New Year's Day, officials said.*

Notes

Notes

Notes

NOTES

NOTES

NOTES

NOTES

NOTES

NOTES

NOTES

NOTES

NOTES

NOTES

www.ingramcontent.com/pod-product-compliance
Lightning Source LLC
Chambersburg PA
CBHW030303130626
46549CB00002B/668